NSSM: 200

THE KISSINGER REPORT

Implications of Worldwide Population
Growth for U.S. Security and Overseas
Interests

Three Documents:

The 1974 National Security Study Memorandum

and

The April 1974 Initiating Memo

and

The NSDM 314 Implementation Memo

NSSM: 200

THE KISSINGER REPORT

Implications of Worldwide Population Growth for U.S. Security and Overseas Interests

Three Documents:

The 1974 National Security Study Memorandum

and

The April 1974 Initiating Memo

and

The NSDM 314 Implementation Memo

Compiled by Dr. Anthony Horvath
Executive Director of the Policy Intersections Research Center
and Reprinted by Suzeteo Enterprises

www.policyintersections.org

ISBN 978-1-936830-69-5

Organization of This Volume

This volume contains three related government documents that have been declassified:

- National Security Study Memorandum 200 Initiating Memo (April, 1974)
- National Security Decision Memorandum 314 (November, 1975)
- National Security Study Memorandum 200 (December, 1974)

The Initiating Memo and NSDM 314 have been presented first because of their brevity.

All three documents appear here exactly in the form they had when declassified and made available to the public, with just two exceptions:

- The Initiating Memo and NSDM 314 have been darkened slightly to make them more readable.
- Inexplicably, the original version of NSSM 200 ceased page numbering after page 33. For the reader's convenience, therefore, page numbers have been placed at the bottom of the page on page 34 and thereafter.

NATIONAL SECURITY COUNCIL
WASHINGTON, D.C. 20506

CONFIDENTIAL - GDS

April 24, 1974

National Security Study Memorandum 200

TO: The Secretary of Defense
            The Secretary of Agriculture
            The Director of Central Intelligence
            The Deputy Secretary of State
            Administrator, Agency for International Development

SUBJECT: Implications of Worldwide Population Growth for U.S.
            Security and Overseas Interests

The President has directed a study of the impact of world population growth
on U.S. security and overseas interests. The study should look forward
at least until the year 2000, and use several alternative reasonable projections of population growth.

In terms of each projection, the study should assess:

     -- the corresponding pace of development, especially in poorer
        countries;

     -- the demand for US exports, especially of food, and the trade pro-
        blems the US may face arising from competition for resources; and

     -- the likelihood that population growth or imbalances will produce
        disruptive foreign policies and international instability.

The study should focus on the international political and economic implications of population growth rather than its ecological, sociological or other
aspects.

The study should then offer possible courses of action for the United States
in dealing with population matters abroad, particularly in developing
countries, with special attention to these questions:

     -- What, if any, new initiatives by the United States are needed to
        focus international attention on the population problem?

     -- Can technological innovations or development reduce growth or
        ameliorate its effects?

CONFIDENTIAL - GDS

- 2 -

   -- Could the United States improve its assistance in the population field and if so, in what form and through which agencies -- bilateral, multilateral, private?

The study should take into account the President's concern that population policy is a human concern intimately related to the dignity of the individual and the objective of the United States is to work closely with others, rather than seek to impose our views on others.

The President has directed that the study be accomplished by the NSC Under Secretaries Committee. The Chairman, Under Secretaries Committee, is requested to forward the study together with the Committee's action recommendations no later than May 29, 1974, for consideration by the President.

Henry A. Kissinger

cc: Chairman, Joint Chiefs of Staff

Gen. Scowcroft

NATIONAL SECURITY COUNCIL
WASHINGTON, D.C. 20506

November 26, 1975

National Security Decision Memorandum 314

TO: The Secretary of State
                 The Secretary of the Treasury
                 The Secretary of Defense
                 The Secretary of Agriculture
                 The Secretary of Health, Education and Welfare
                 The Administrator, Agency for International Development

SUBJECT: Implications of Worldwide Population Growth for United
                 States Security and Overseas Interests

The President has reviewed the interagency response to NSSM 200
and the covering memorandum from the Chairman of the NSC Under
Secretaries Committee   He believes that United States leadership
is essential to combat population growth, to implement the World
Population Plan of Action and to advance United States security and
overseas interests.   The President endorses the policy recommendations contained in the Executive Summary of the NSSM 200 response,
with the following observations and exceptions:

AID Programs

Care must be taken that our AID program efforts are not so diffuse
as to have little impact upon those countries contributing the largest
growth in population, and where reductions in fertility are most
needed for economic and social progress.

Research and Evaluation

An examination should be undertaken of the effectiveness of population
control programs in countries at all levels of development, but with

emphasis on the LDC's. The examination should include an evaluation of AID program efforts as well as other efforts by national or international groups. The study would attempt to determine the separate effect of the population program, taking account of other economic or social factors which may have also influenced fertility.

Research on broader issues should be undertaken examining the factors affecting change (or lack of change) in the birth rate in different countries.

Funding for Population Programs:

The President desires that a review be undertaken quickly to examine specific recommendations for funding in the population assistance and family planning field for the period after FY 1976. The President wishes a detailed analysis of the recommended funding levels in the NSSM 200 study bearing in mind his desire to advance population goals. This analysis should include performance criteria to assure that any additional funds are utilized in the most effective manner. The appropriate level of funding of multilateral programs which effectively support this objective should be included in this review. The Chairman of the USC is responsible for preparing this analysis which is due 60 days from the date of this NSDM.

The Role of Other Countries:

Emphasis should be given to fostering international cooperation in reducing population growth in pursuing the recommendations of the World Population Plan of Action. It is important to enlist additional contributions from other developed and newly rich countries for bilateral and multilateral programs.

Basic Approach to Developing Countries' Population Programs:

Leaders of key developing countries should be encouraged to support national and multilateral population assistance programs.

The objective of the United States in this field is to work closely with others rather than to seek to impose our views on others. Our efforts should stress the linkage between reduced population growth and the resultant economic and social gains for the poorest nations. In all these efforts, we should recognize the basic dignity of the individual and his or her right to choose freely family goals and family planning alternatives.

National and World Population Goals:

The President believes that the recommendation contained in paragraph 31(c) of the Executive Summary dealing with the announcement of a United States national goal is outside the scope of NSSM 200. Of course, domestic efforts in this field must continue in order to achieve worldwide recognition that the United States has been successfully practicing the basic recommendations of the World Plan of Action and that the nation's birthrate is below the replacement level of fertility. In order to obtain the support of the United States citizens for our involvement in international population programs, it is important that they recognize that excessive world population growth can affect domestic problems including economic expansion as well as world instability.

Concerning the consideration of World Population Goals in paragraph 31(b), it should be understood that the general goal of achieving global replacement levels of fertility by the year 2000 does not imply interference in the national policies of other countries.

The Under Secretaries Committee, in conjunction with all appropriate agencies of the Executive Branch, may wish to make further recommendations to the President on these subjects.

Coordination of United States Global Population Policy:

Implementation of a United States worldwide population strategy will involve careful coordination. The response to NSSM 200 is a good beginning, but as noted above, there is need for further examination of the mix of United States assistance strategy and its most efficient application.

The President, therefore, assigns to the Chairman, NSC Under Secretaries Committee, the responsibility to define and develop policy in the population field and to coordinate its implementation beyond the NSSM 200 response.

National Security Study Memorandum

NSSM 200

Implications of Worldwide Population Growth
For U.S. Security and Overseas Interests
(THE KISSINGER REPORT)

December 10, 1974

CLASSIFIED BY Harry C. Blaney, III
SUBJECT TO GENERAL DECLASSIFICATION SCHEDULE
OF EXECUTIVE ORDER 11652 AUTOMATICALLY DOWN-
GRADED AT TWO YEAR INTERVALS AND DECLASSIFIED
ON DECEMBER 31, 1980.

This document can only be declassified by the White House.

TABLE OF CONTENTS

EXECUTIVE SUMARY

World Demographic Trends

1. World population growth since World War 11 is quantitatively and qualitatively different from any previous epoch in human history. The rapid reduction in death rates, unmatched by corresponding birth rate reductions, has brought total growth rates close to 2 percent a year, compared with about 1 percent before World War II, under 0.5 percent in 1750-1900, and far lower rates before 1750. The effect is to double the world's population in 35 years instead of 100 years. Almost 80 million are now being added each year, compared with 10 million in 1900.

2. The second new feature of population trends is the sharp differentiation between rich and poor countries. Since 1950, population in the former group has been growing at O to 1.5 percent per year, and in the latter at 2.0 to 3.5 percent (doubling in 20 to 35 years). Some of the highest rates of increase are in areas already densely populated and with a weak resource base.

3. Because of the momentum of population dynamics, reductions in birth rates affect total numbers only slowly. High birth rates in the recent past have resulted in a high proportion m the youngest age groups, so that there will continue to be substantial population increases over many years even if a two-child family should become the norm in the future. Policies to reduce fertility will have their main effects on total numbers only after several decades. However, if future numbers are to be kept within reasonable bounds, it is urgent that measures to reduce fertility be started and made effective in the 1970's and 1980's. Moreover, programs started now to reduce birth rates will have short run advantages for developing countries in lowered demands on food, health and educational and other services and in enlarged capacity to contribute to productive investments, thus accelerating development.

4. U.N. estimates use the 3.6 billion population of 1970 as a base (there are nearly 4 billion now) and project from about 6 billion to 8 billion people for the year 2000 with the U.S. medium estimate at 6.4 billion. The U.S. medium projections show a world population of 12 billion by 2075 which implies a five-fold increase in south and southeast Asia and in Latin American and a seven-fold increase in Africa, compared with a doubling in east Asia and a 40% increase in the presently developed countries (see Table I). Most demographers, including the U.N. and the U.S. Population Council, regard the range of 10 to 13 billion as the most likely level for world population stability, even with intensive efforts at fertility control. (These figures assume, that sufficient food could be produced and distributed to avoid limitation through famines.)

Adequacy of World Food Supplies

5. Growing populations will have a serious impact on the need for food especially in the poorest, fastest growing LDCs. While under normal weather conditions and assuming food production growth in line with recent trends, total world agricultural production could expand faster than population, there will nevertheless be serious problems in food distribution and financing, making shortages, even at today's poor nutrition levels, probable in many of the larger more populous LDC regions. Even today 10 to 20 million people die each year due, directly or indirectly, to malnutrition. Even more serious is the consequence of major crop failures which are likely to occur from time to time.

6. The most serious consequence for the short and middle term is the possibility of massive famines in certain parts of the world, especially the poorest regions. World needs for food rise by 2-1/2 percent or more per year (making a modest allowance for improved diets and nutrition) at a time when readily available fertilizer and well-watered land is already largely being utilized. Therefore, additions to food production must come mainly from higher yields. Countries with large population growth cannot afford constantly growing imports, but for them to raise food output steadily by 2 to 4 percent over the next generation or two is a formidable challenge. Capital and foreign exchange requirements for intensive agriculture are heavy, and are aggravated by energy cost increases and fertilizer scarcities and price rises. The institutional, technical, and economic problems of transforming traditional agriculture are also very difficult to overcome.

7. In addition, in some overpopulated regions, rapid population growth presses on a fragile environment in ways that threaten longer-term food production: through cultivation of marginal lands, overgrazing, desertification, deforestation, and soil erosion, with consequent destruction of land and pollution of water, rapid siltation of reservoirs, and impairment of inland and coastal fisheries.

Mineral and Fuel

8. Rapid population growth is not in itself a major factor in pressure on depletable resources (fossil fuels and other minerals), since demand for them depends more on levels of industrial output than on numbers of people. On the other hand, the world is increasingly dependent on mineral supplies from developing countries, and if rapid population frustrates their prospects for economic development and social progress, the resulting instability may undermine the conditions for expanded output and sustained flows of such resources.

9. There will be serious problems for some of the poorest LDCs with rapid population growth. They will increasingly find it difficult to pay for needed raw materials and energy. Fertilizer, vital for their own agricultural production, will be difficult to obtain for the next few years. Imports for fuel and other materials will cause grave problems which could impinge on the U.S., both through the need to supply greater financial support and in LDC efforts to obtain

better terms of trade through higher prices for exports.

Economic Development and Population Growth

10. Rapid population growth creates a severe drag on rates of economic development otherwise attainable, sometimes to the point of preventing any increase in per capita incomes. In addition to the overall impact on per capita incomes, rapid population growth seriously affects a vast range of other aspects of the quality of life important to social and economic progress in the LDCs.

11. Adverse economic factors which generally result from rapid population growth include:

-- reduced family savings and domestic investment;

-- increased need for large amounts of foreign exchange for food imports;

-- intensification of severe unemployment and underemployment;

-- the need for large expenditures for services such as dependency support, education, and health which would be used for more productive investment;
-- the concentration of developmental resources on increasing food production to ensure survival for a larger population, rather than on improving living conditions for smaller total numbers.

12. While GNP increased per annum at an average rate of 5 percent in LDCs over the last decade, the population increase of 2.5 percent reduced the average annual per capita growth rate to only 2.5 percent. In many heavily populated areas this rate was 2 percent or less. In the LDCs hardest hit by the oil crisis, with an aggregate population of 800 million, GNP increases   may be reduced to less than 1 percent per capita per year for the remainder of the 1970's. For the poorest half of the populations of these countries, with average incomes of less than $100, the prospect is for no growth or retrogression for this period.

13. If significant progress can be made in slowing population growth, the positive impact on growth of GNP and per capita income will be significant. Moreover, economic and social progress will probably contribute further to the decline in fertility rates.

14. High birth rates appear to stem primarily from:

a.   inadequate information about and availability of means of fertility control;

b.   inadequate motivation for reduced numbers of children combined with motivation for many children resulting from still high infant and child mortality and need for support in old age; and

c.   the slowness of change in family preferences in response to changes in environment.

15. The universal objective of increasing the world's standard of living dictates that economic growth outpace population growth. In many high population growth areas of the world, the largest proportion of GNP is consumed, with only a small amount saved. Thus, a small proportion of GNP is available for investment - the "engine" of economic growth. Most experts agree that, with fairly constant costs per acceptor, expenditures on effective family planning services are generally one of the most cost effective investments for an LDC country seeking to improve overall welfare and per capita economic growth. We cannot wait for overall modernization and development to produce lower fertility rates naturally since this will undoubtedly take many decades in most developing countries, during which time rapid population growth will tend to slow development and widen even more the gap between rich and poor.

16. The interrelationships between development and population growth are complex and not wholly understood. Certain aspects of economic development and modernization appear to be more directly related to lower birth rates than others. Thus certain development programs may bring a faster demographic transition to lower fertility rates than other aspects of development. The World Population Plan of Action adopted at the World Population Conference recommends that countries working to affect fertility levels should give priority to development programs and health and education strategies which have a decisive effect on fertility. International cooperation should give priority to assisting such national efforts. These programs include: (a) improved health care and nutrition to reduce child mortality, (b) education and improved social status for women; (c) increased female employment; (d) improved old-age security; and (e) assistance for the rural poor, who generally have the highest fertility, with actions to redistribute income and resources including providing privately owned farms. However, one cannot proceed simply from identification of relationships to specific large-scale operational programs. For example, we do not yet know of cost-effective ways to encourage increased female employment, particularly if we are concerned about not adding to male unemployment. We do not yet know what specific packages of programs will be most cost effective in many situations.

17. There is need for more information on cost effectiveness of different approaches on both the "supply" and the "demand" side of the picture. On the supply side, intense efforts are required to assure full availability by 1980 of birth control information and means to all (fertile individuals, especially in rural areas. Improvement is also needed in methods of birth control most) acceptable and useable by the rural poor. On the demand side, further experimentation and implementation action projects and programs are needed. In particular, more research is needed on the motivation of the poorest who often have the highest fertility rates. Assistance programs must be more precisely targeted to this group than in the past.

18. It may well be that desired family size will not decline to near replacement levels until the lot of the LDC rural poor improves to the extent that the benefits of reducing family size

appear to them to outweigh the costs. For urban people, a rapidly growing element in the LDCs, the liabilities of having too many children are already becoming apparent. Aid recipients and donors must also emphasize development and improvements in the quality of life of the poor, if significant progress is to be made in controlling population growth. Although it was adopted primarily for other reasons, the new emphasis of AID's legislation on problems of the poor (which is echoed in comparable changes in policy emphasis by other donors and by an increasing number of LDC's) is directly relevant to the conditions required for fertility reduction.

Political Effects of Population Factors

19. The political consequences of current population factors in the LDCs - rapid growth, internal migration, high percentages of young people, slow improvement in living standards, urban concentrations, and pressures for foreign migration — are damaging to the internal stability and international relations of countries in whose advancement the U.S. is interested, thus creating political or even national security problems for the U.S. In a broader sense, there is a major risk of severe damage to world economic, political, and ecological systems and, as these systems begin to fail, to our humanitarian values.

20. The pace of internal migration from countryside to over swollen cities is greatly intensified by rapid population growth. Enormous burdens are placed on LDC governments for public administration, sanitation, education, police, and other services, and urban slum dwellers (though apparently not recent migrants) may serve as a volatile, violent force which threatens political stability.

21. Adverse socio-economic conditions generated by these and related factors may contribute to high and increasing levels of child abandonment, juvenile delinquency, chronic and growing underemployment and unemployment, petty thievery, organized brigandry, food riots, separatist movements, communal massacres, revolutionary actions and counter-revolutionary coupe. Such conditions also detract form the environment needed to attract the foreign capital vital to increasing levels of economic growth in these areas. If these conditions result in expropriation of foreign interests, such action, from an economic viewpoint, is not in the best interests of either the investing country or the host government.

22. In international relations, population factors are crucial in, and often determinants of, violent conflicts in developing areas. Conflicts that are regarded in primarily political terms often have demographic roots. Recognition of these relationships appears crucial to any understanding or prevention of such hostilities.

General Goals and Requirements for Dealing With Rapid Population Growth

23. The central question for world population policy in the year 1974, is whether mankind is to remain on a track toward an ultimate population of 12 to 15 billion -- implying a five to seven-fold increase in almost all the underdeveloped world outside of China -- or whether (despite the momentum of population growth) it can be switched over to the course of

earliest feasible population stability -- implying ultimate totals of 8 to 9 billions and not more than a three or four-fold increase in any major region.

24. What are the stakes? We do not know whether technological developments will make it possible to feed over 8 much less 12 billion people in the 21st century. We cannot be entirely certain that climatic changes in the coming decade will not create great difficulties in feeding a growing population, especially people in the LDCs who live under increasingly marginal and more vulnerable conditions. There exists at least the possibility that present developments point toward Malthusian conditions for many regions of the world.

25. But even if survival for these much larger numbers is possible, it will in all likelihood be bare survival, with all efforts going in the good years to provide minimum nutrition and utter dependence in the bad years on emergency rescue efforts from the less populated and richer countries of the world. In the shorter run -- between now and the year 2000 -- the difference between the two courses can be some perceptible material gain in the crowded poor regions, and some improvement in the relative distribution of intra- country per capita income between rich and poor, as against permanent poverty and the widening of income gaps. A much more vigorous effort to slow population growth can also mean a very great difference between enormous tragedies of malnutrition and starvation as against only serious chronic conditions.

Policy Recommendations

26. There is no single approach which will "solve" the population problem. The complex social and economic factors involved call for a comprehensive strategy with both bilateral and multilateral elements. At the same time actions and programs must be tailored to specific countries and groups. Above all, LDCs themselves must play the most important role to achieve success.

27. Coordination among the bilateral donors and multilateral organizations is vital to any effort to moderate population growth. Each kind of effort will be needed for worldwide results.

28. World policy and programs in the population field should incorporate two major objectives:

(a)   actions to accommodate continued population growth up to 6 billions by the mid-21st century without massive starvation or total frustration of developmental hopes; and

(b)   actions to keep the ultimate level as close as possible to 8 billions rather than permitting it to reach 10 billions, 13 billions, or more.

29. While specific goals in this area are difficult to state, our aim should be for the world to achieve a replacement level of fertility, (a two- child family on the average), by about the year

2000. This will require the present 2 percent growth rate to decline to 1.7 percent within a decade and to 1.1 percent by 2000 compared to the U.N medium projection, this goal would result in 500 million fewer people in 2000 and about 3 billion fewer in 2050. Attainment of this goal will require greatly intensified population programs. A basis for developing national population growth control targets to achieve this world target is contained in the World Population Plan of Action.

30. The World Population Plan of Action is not self-enforcing and will require vigorous efforts by interested countries, U.N. agencies and other international bodies to make it effective. U.S. leadership is essential. The strategy must include the following elements and actions:

(a)   Concentration on key countries.
       Assistance for population moderation should give primary emphasis to the largest and fastest growing developing countries where there is special U.S. political and strategic interest. Those countries are: India, Bangladesh, Pakistan, Nigeria, Mexico, Indonesia, Brazil, the Philippines, Thailand, Egypt, Turkey, Ethiopia and Columbia. Together, they account for 47 percent of the world's current population increase. (It should be recognized that at present AID bilateral assistance to some of these countries may not be acceptable.) Bilateral assistance, to the extent that funds are available, will be given to other countries, considering such factors as population growth, need for external assistance, long-term U.S. interests and willingness to engage in self help. Multilateral programs must necessarily have a wider coverage and the bilateral programs of other national donors will be shaped to their particular interests. At the same time, the U.S. will look to the multilateral agencies, especially the U.N. Fund for Population Activities which already has projects in over 80 countries to increase population assistance on a broader basis with increased U.S. contributions. This is desirable in terms of U.S. interests and necessary in political terms in the United Nations. But progress nevertheless, must be made in the key 13 and our limited resources should give major emphasis to them.

(b)   Integration of population factors and population programs into country development planning. As called for the world Population Plan of Action, developing countries and those aiding them should specifically take population factors into account in national planning and include population programs in such plans.

(c)   Increased assistance for family planning services, information and technology. This is a vital aspect of any world population program.
       1) Family planning information and materials based on present technology should be made fully available as rapidly as possible to the 85 % of the populations in key LDCs not now reached, essentially rural poor who have the highest fertility.

2) Fundamental and evelopmental research should be expanded, aimed at simple, low-cost, effective, safe, long-lasting and acceptable methods of fertility control. Support by all federal agencies for biomedical research in this field should be increased by $60 million annually.

(d)   Creating conditions conducive to fertility decline. For its own merits and consistent with the   recommendations of the World Population Plan of Action, priority should be given in the general aid program to selective development policies in sectors offering the greatest promise of increased motivation for smaller family size. In many cases pilot programs and experimental research will be needed as guidance for later efforts on a larger scale. The preferential sectors include:

-- Providing minimal levels of education, especially for women;

-- Reducing infant mortality, including through simple low cost health care networks;

-- Expanding wage employment, especially for women;

-- Developing alternatives to children as a source of old age security;

-- Increasing income of the poorest, especially in rural areas, including providing privately owned farms;

-- Education of new generations on the desirability of smaller families.

While AID has information on the relative importance of the new major socio- economic factors that lead to lower birth rates, much more research and experimentation need to be done to determine what cost effective programs and policy will lead to lower birth rates.

(e)   Food and agricultural assistance is vital for any population sensitive development strategy. The provision of adequate food stocks for a   growing population in times of shortage is crucial. Without such a program   for the LDCs there is considerable chance that such shortage will lead to conflict and adversely affect population goals and developmental efforts.   Specific recommendations are included in Section IV (c) of this study.

(f)   Development of a worldwide political and popular commitment to population stabilization is fundamental to any effective strategy.
        This requires the support and commitment of key LDC leaders. This will only take place if they clearly see the negative impact of unrestricted population growth and believe it is possible to deal with this question through governmental action.

The U.S. should encourage LDC leaders to take the lead in advancing family planning and population stabilization both within multilateral organizations and through bilateral contacts with other LDCs. This will require that the President and the Secretary of State treat the subject of population growth control as a matter of paramount importance and address it specifically in their regular contacts with leaders of other governments, particularly LDCs.

31. The World Population Plan of Action and the resolutions adopted by consensus by 137 nations at the August 1974 U.N. World Population Conference, though not ideal, provide an excellent framework for developing a worldwide system of population/ family planning programs. We should use them to generate U.N. agency and national leadership for an all-out effort to lower growth rates. Constructive action by the U.S. will further our objectives. To this end we should:

(a)   Strongly support the World Population Plan of Action and the adoption of its appropriate provisions in national and other programs.

(b)   Urge the adoption by national programs of specific population goals including replacement levels of fertility for DCs and LDCs by 2000.

(c)   After suitable preparation in the U.S., announce a U.S. goal to maintain our present national average fertility no higher than replacement level and attain near stability by 2000.

(d)   Initiate an international cooperative strategy of national research programs on human reproduction and fertility control covering biomedical and socio-economic factors, as proposed by the U.S. Delegation at Bucharest.

(e)   Act on our offer at Bucharest to collaborate with other interested donors and U.N. agencies to aid selected countries to develop low cost preventive health and family planning services.

(f)   Work directly with donor countries and through the U.N. Fund for Population Activities and the OECD/DAC to increase bilateral and multilateral assistance for population programs.

32. As measures to increase understanding of population factors by LDC leaders and to strengthen population planning in national development plans, we should carry out the recommendations in Part II, Section VI, including:

(a)   Consideration of population factors and population policies in all Country Assistance Strategy Papers (CASP) and Development Assistance Program (DAP) multi-year strategy papers.

(b)   Prepare projections of population growth individualized for countries with analyses of development of each country and discuss them with national leaders.

(c)   Provide for greatly increased training programs for senior officials of LDCs in the elements of demographic economics.

(d)   Arrange for familiarization programs at U.N. Headquarters in New York for ministers of governments, senior policy level officials and comparably influential leaders from private life.

(e)   Assure assistance to LDC leaders in integrating population factors in national plans, particularly as they relate to health services, education, agricultural resources and development, employment, equitable distribution of income and social stability.

(f)   Also assure assistance to LDC leaders in relating population policies and family planning programs to major sectors of development health, nutrition, agriculture, education, social services, organized labour, women's activities, and community development.

(g)   Undertake initiatives to implement the Percy Amendment regarding improvement in the status of women.

(h)   Give emphasis in assistance to programs on development of rural areas.

Beyond these activities which are essentially directed at national interests, we must assure that a broader educational concept is developed to convey an acute understanding to national leaders of the interrelation of national interests and world population growth.

33. We must take care that our activities should not give the appearance to the LDCs of an industrialized country policy directed against the LDCs. Caution must be taken that in any approaches in this field we support in the LDCs are ones we can support within this country. "Third World" leaders should be in the forefront and obtain the credit for successful programs. In this context it is important to demonstrate to LDC leaders that such family planning programs have worked and can work within a reasonable period of time.

34. To help assure others of our intentions we should indicate our emphasis on the right of individuals and couples to determine freely and responsibly the number and spacing of their children and to have information, education and means to do so, and our continued interest in improving the overall general welfare. We should use the authority provided by the World Population Plan of Action to advance the principles that: 1) responsibility in parenthood includes responsibility to the children and the community and 2) that nations in exercising their sovereignty to set population policies should take into account the welfare of their neighbours

and the world. To strengthen the worldwide approach, family planning programs should be supported by multilateral organizations wherever they can provide the most efficient means.

35. To support such family planning and related development assistance efforts there is need to increase public and leadership information in this field. We recommend increased emphasis on mass media, newer communications technology and other population education and motivation programs by the UN and USIA. Higher priority should be given to these information programs in this field worldwide.

36. In order to provide the necessary resources and leadership, support by the U.S. public and Congress will be necessary. A significant amount of funds will be required for a number of years. High level personal contact by the Secretary of State and other officials on the subject at an early date with Congressional counterparts is needed. A program for this purpose should be developed by OES with H and AID.

37. There is an alternative view which holds that a growing number of experts believe that the population situation is already more serious and less amenable to solution through voluntary measures than is generally accepted. It holds that, to prevent even more widespread food shortage and other demographic catastrophes than are generally anticipated, even stronger measures are required and some fundamental, very difficult moral issues need to be addressed. These include, for example, our own consumption patterns, mandatory programs, tight control of our food resources. In view of the seriousness of these issues, explicit consideration of them should begin in the Executive Branch, the Congress and the U.N. soon. (See the end of Section I for this viewpoint.)

38. Implementing the actions discussed above (in paragraphs 1-36), will require a significant expansion in AID funds for population/family planning. A number of major actions in the area of creating conditions for fertility decline can be funded from resources available to the sectors in question (e.g., education, agriculture). Other actions, including family planning services, research and experimental activities on factors effecting fertility, come under population funds. We recommend increases in AID budget requests to the Congress on the order of $35-50 million annually through FY 1980 (above the $137.5 million requested for FY 1975). This funding would cover both bilateral programs and contributions to multilateral organizations. However, the level of funds needed in the future could change significantly, depending on such factors as major breakthroughs in fertility control technologies and LDC receptivities to population assistance. To help develop, monitor, and evaluate the expanded actions discussed above, AID is likely to need additional direct hire personnel in the population/family planning area. As a corollary to expanded AID funding levels for population, efforts must be made to encourage increased contributions by other donors and recipient countries to help reduce rapid population growth.

Policy Follow-up and Coordination

39. This world wide population strategy involves very complex and difficult questions.

Its implementation will require very careful coordination and specific application in individual circumstances. Further work is greatly needed in examining the mix of our assistance strategy and its most efficient application. A number of agencies are interested and involved. Given this, there appears to be a need for a better and higher level mechanism to refine and develop policy in this field and to coordinate its implementation beyond this NSSM. The following options are suggested for consideration:

(a) That the NSC Under Secretaries Committee be given responsibility for policy and executive review of this subject:

Pros:

- Because of the major foreign policy implications of the recommended population strategy a high level focus on policy is required for the success of such a major effort.

- With the very wide agency interests in this topic there is need for an accepted and normal inter agency process for effective analysis and disinterested policy development and implementation within the N.S.C. system.
- Staffing support for implementation of the NSSM-200 follow-on exists within the USC framework including utilization of the Office of Population of the Department of State as well as others.

- USC has provided coordination and follow-up in major foreign policy areas involving a number of agencies as is the case in this study.

Cons:

- The USC would not be within the normal policy-making framework for development policy as would be in the case with the DCC.

- The USC is further removed from the process of budget development and review of the AID Population Assistance program.

(b) That when its establishment is authorized by the President, - the Development Coordination Committee, headed by the AID Administrator be given overall responsibility:

* NOTE: AID expects the DCC will have the following composition: The Administrator of AID as Chairman; the Under Secretary of State for Economic Affairs; the Under Secretary of Treasury for Monetary Affairs; the Under Secretaries of Commerce, Agriculture and labour; an Associate Director of OMB; the Executive Director of CIEP, STR; a representative of the NSC; the President of the EX-IM Bank and OPIC; and any other agency when items of interest to them are under discussion.

Pros: *(Provided by AID)*

- It is precisely for coordination of this type of development issue involving a variety of U.S. policies toward LDCs that the Congress directed the establishment of the DCC.

- The DCC is also the body best able to relate population issues to other development issues, with which they are intimately related.

- The DCC has the advantage of stressing technical and financial aspects of U.S. population policies, thereby minimizing political complications frequently inherent in population programs.

- It is, in AID's view, the coordinating body best located to take an overview of all the population activities now taking place under bilateral and multilateral auspices.

Cons:

- While the DCC will doubtless have substantial technical competence, the entire range of political and other factors bearing on our global population strategy might be more effectively considered by a group having a broader focus than the DCC.

- The DCC is not within the N.S.C. system which provides more direct access to both the President and the principal foreign policy decision-making mechanism.

- The DCC might overly emphasize purely developmental aspects of population and under emphasize other important elements.

(c)   <u>That the NSC/CEP be asked to lead an Interdepartmental Group for this subject to insure follow-up interagency coordination, and further policy development</u>. (No participating Agency supports this option, therefore it is only included to present a full range of possibilities).

Option (a) is supported by State, Treasury,
Defence (ISA and JCS),
Agriculture, HEW, Commerce NSC and CIA
Option (b) is supported by AID.

Under any of the above options, there should be an annual review of our population policy to examine progress, insure our programs are in keeping with the latest information in this field, identify possible deficiencies, and recommend additional action at the appropriate level5

1. Department of Commerce supports the option of placing the population policy formulation mechanism under the auspices of the USC but believes that any detailed economic questions resulting from proposed population policies be explored through existing domestic and international economic policy channels.

2 . AID believes these reviews undertaken only periodically might look at selected areas or at the entire range of population policy depending on problems and needs which arise.

Table 1. POPULATION GROWTH, BY MAJOR REGION: 1970_2075
(Absolute numbers in billions)

| | 1970 Actual | U.N. Medium Variant Projections for: | | | | U.S. Proposed Goal... for World Population Plan of Action Projection for: | | | |
| | | 2000 | | 2075 | | 2000 | | 2075 | |
		Numbers	Multiple of 1970	Numbers	Multiple of 1970	Numbers	Multiple of 1970	Numbers	Multiple of 1970
WORLD TOTAL	3.6	6.4	x 1.8	12.0	x 3.3	5.9	1.6	8.4	x 2.3
More Developed Regions	1.1	1.4	x 1.3	1.6	x 1.45	1.4	x 1.2	1.6	x 1.4
Less Developed Regions	2.5	5.0	x 2.0	10.5	x 4.1	4.5	x 1.8	6.7	x 2.65
Africa	0.4	0.8	x 2.4	2.3	x 6.65	0.6	x 1.8	0.9	x 2.70
East Asia	0.8	1.2*	x 1.5	1.6*	x 2.0	1.4*	x 1.6	1.9	x 2.30
South & South East Asia	1.1	2.4	x 2.1	5.3	x 4.7	2.1	x 1.9	3.2	x 2.85
Latin America	0.2	0.6	x 2.3	1.2	x 5.0	0.5	x 2.0	0.7	x 3.00

More Developed Regions: Europe, North America, Japan, Australia, New Zealand and Temperate South America.
Less Developed Regions: All other regions

*The seeming inconsistency in growth trends between the UN medium and the US_Proposed Projection variants for   East Asia is due to a
lack of reliable information on China's total population, its age structure, and the achievements   of the country's birth control program.

CHAPTER I - WORLD DEMOGRAPHIC TRENDS

Introduction

The present world population growth is unique. Rates of increase are much higher than in earlier centuries, they are more widespread, and have a greater effect on economic life, social justice, and -- quite likely -- on public order and political stability. The significance of population growth is enhanced because it comes at a time when the absolute size and rate of increase of the global economy, need for agricultural land, demand for and consumption of resources including water, production of wastes and pollution have also escalated to historically unique levels. Factors that only a short time ago were considered separately now have interlocking relationships, inter- dependence in a literal sense. The changes are not only quantitatively greater than in the past but qualitatively different. The growing burden is not only on resources but on administrative and social institutions as well.

Population growth is, of course, only one of the important factors in this new, highly integrated tangle of relationships. However, it differs from the others because it is a determinant of the demand sector while others relate to output and supply. (Population growth also contributes to supply through provision of manpower; in most developing countries, however, the problem is not a lack of but a surfeit of hands.) It is, therefore, most pervasive, affecting what needs to be done in regard to other factors. Whether other problems can be solved depends, in varying degrees, on the extent to which rapid population growth and other population variables can be brought under control.

Highlights of Current Demographic Trends

Since 1950, world population has been undergoing unprecedented growth. This growth has four prominent features:

1. It is unique, far more rapid than ever in history.

2. It is much more rapid in less developed than in developed regions.

3. Concentration in towns and cities is increasing much more rapidly than overall population growth and is far more rapid in LDCs than in developed countries.

4. It has a tremendous built-in momentum that will inexorably double populations of most less developed countries by 2000 and will treble or quadruple their populations before levelling off -- unless far greater efforts at fertility control are made than are being made.

Therefore, if a country wants to influence its total numbers through population policy, it must act in the immediate future in order to make a substantial difference in the long run.

For most of man's history, world population grew very slowly. At the rate of growth estimated for the first 18 centuries A.D., it required more than 1,000 years for world population to double in size. With the beginnings of the industrial revolution and of modern medicine and sanitation over two hundred years ago, population growth rates began to accelerate. At the current growth rate (1.9 percent) world population will double in 37 years.

--By about 1830, world population reached 1 billion. The second billion was added in about 100 years by 1930. The third billion in 30 years by 1960. The fourth will be reached in 1975.

--Between 1750-1800 less than 4 million were being added, on the average, to the earth's population each year. Between 1850-1900, it was close to 8 million. By 1950 it had grown to 40 million. By 1975 it will be about 80 million.

In the developed countries of Europe, growth rates in the last century rarely exceeded 1.0-1.2 percent per year, almost never 1.5 percent. Death rates were much higher than in most LDCs today. In North America where growth rates were higher, immigration made a significant contribution. In nearly every country of Europe, growth rates are now below 1 percent, in many below 0.5 percent. The natural growth rate (births minus deaths) in the United States is less than 0.6 percent. Including immigration (the world's highest) it is less than 0.7 percent.

In less developed countries growth rates average about 2.4 percent. For the People's Republic of China, with a massive, enforced birth control program, the growth rate is estimated at under 2 percent. India's is variously estimated from 2.2 percent, Brazil at 2.8 percent, Mexico at 3.4 percent, and Latin America at about 2.9 percent. African countries, with high birth as well as high death rates, average 2.6 percent; this growth rate will increase as death rates go down.

The world's population is now about 3.9 billion; 1.1 billion in the developed countries (30 percent) and 2.8 billion in the less developed countries (70 percent).

In 1950, only 28 percent of the world's population or 692 million, lived in urban localities. Between 1950 and 1970, urban population expanded at a rate twice as rapid as the rate of growth of total population. In 1970, urban population increased to 36 percent of world total and numbered 1.3 billion. By 2000, according to the UN's medium variant projection, 3.2 billion (about half of the total) of world inhabitants will live in cities and towns.

In developed countries, the urban population varies from 45 to 85 percent; in LDCs, it varies from close to zero in some African states to nearly 100 percent in Hong Kong and Singapore.

In LDCs, urban population is projected to more than triple the remainder of this century, from 622 million in 1970 to 2,087 in 2000. Its proportion in total LDC population will thus increase from 25 percent in 1970 to 41 percent in 2000. This implies that by the end of this

century LDCs will reach half the level of urbanization projected for DCs (82 percent) (See Appendix Table 1).

The enormous built-in momentum of population growth in the less developed countries (and to a degree in the developed countries) is, if possible, even more important and ominous than current population size and rates of growth. Unlike a conventional explosion, population growth provides a continuing chain reaction. This momentum springs from (1) high fertility levels of LDC populations and (2) the very high percentage of maturing young people in populations. The typical developed country, Sweden for example, may have 25% of the population under 15 years of age. The typical developing country has 41% to 45% of its population under 15. This means that a tremendous number of future parents, compared to existing parents, are already born. Even if they have fewer children per family than their parents, the increase in population will be very great.

Three projections (not predictions), based on three different assumptions concerning fertility, will illustrate the generative effect of this building momentum.

a. Present fertility continued: If present fertility rates were to remain constant, the 1974 population 3.9 billion would increase to 7.8 billion by the hear 2000 and rise to a theoretical 103 billion by 2075.

b. U.N. "Medium Variant": If present birth rates in the developing countries, averaging about 38/1000 were further reduced to 29/1000 by 2000, the world's population in 2000 would be 6.4 billion, with over 100 million being added each year. At the time stability (non-growth) is reached in about 2100, world population would exceed 12.0 billion.

c. Replacement Fertility by 2000: If replacement levels of fertility were reached by 2000, the world's population in 2000 would be 5.9 billion and at the time of stability, about 2075, would be 8.4 billion. ("Replacement level" of fertility is not zero population growth. It is the level of fertility when couples are limiting their families to an average of about two children. For most countries, where there are high percentages of young people, even the attainment of replacement levels of fertility means that the population will continue to grow for additional 50-60 years to much higher numbers before levelling off.)

It is reasonable to assume that projection (a) is unreal since significant efforts are already being made to slow population growth and because even the most extreme pro-natalists do not argue that the earth could or should support 103 billion people. Famine, pestilence, war, or birth control will stop population growth far short of this figure.

The UN medium variant (projection (b) has been described in a publication of the UN

Population Division as "a synthesis of the results of efforts by demographers of the various countries and the UN Secretariat to formulate realistic assumptions with regard to future trends, in view of information about present conditions and past experiences." Although by no means infallible, these projections provide plausible working numbers and are used by UN agencies (e.g., FAO, ILO) for their specialized analyses. One major shortcoming of most projections, however, is that "information about present conditions" quoted above is not quite up-to-date. Even in the United States, refined fertility and mortality rates become available only after a delay of several years.

Thus, it is possible that the rate of world population growth has actually fallen below (or for that matter increased from) that assumed under the UN medium variant. A number of less developed countries with rising living levels (particularly with increasing equality of income) and efficient family planning programs have experienced marked declines in fertility. Where access to family planning services has been restricted, fertility levels can be expected to show little change.

It is certain that fertility rates have already fallen significantly in Hong King, Singapore, Taiwan, Fiji, South Korea, Barbados, Chile, Costa Rica, Trinidad and Tobago, and Mauritius (See Table 1). Moderate declines have also been registered in West Malaysia, Sri Lanka, and Egypt. Steady increases in the number of acceptors at family planning facilities indicate a likelihood of some fertility reduction in Thailand, Indonesia, the Philippines, Colombia, and other countries which have family planning programs. On the other hand, there is little concrete evidence of significant fertility reduction in the populous countries of India, Bangladesh, Pakistan, etc. 1/ make a serious effort to do something about it.

The differences in the size of total population projected under the three variants become substantial in a relatively short time.

By 1985, the medium variant projects some 342 million fewer people than the constant fertility variant and the replacement variant is 75 million lower than the medium variant.

By the year 2000 the difference between constant and medium fertility variants rises to 1.4 billion and between the medium and replacement variants, close to 500 million. By the year 2000, the span between the high and low series -- some 1.9 billion -- would amount to almost half the present world population.

Most importantly, perhaps, by 2075 the constant variant would have swamped the earth and the difference between the medium and replacement variants would amount to 3.7 billion. (Table 2.)

1/ Of 82 countries for which crude birth rates are available for 1960 and 1972 -- or 88 percent -- experienced a decline in birth rates during this period. The 72 countries include 29 developed countries and 24 independent territories, including Hong Kong and Puerto Rico. The 19 sovereign LDCs include Mexico, Guatemala, El Salvador, Panama, Jamaica, Tunisia, Costa Rica, Chile, Fiji, Mauritius, Trinidad and Tobago, Singapore, Barbados, Taiwan, Egypt, Sri Lanka, Guyana, West Malaysia, and Algeria. (ISPC, US Bureau of the Census).

The significance of the alternative variants is that they reflect the difference between a manageable situation and potential chaos with widespread starvation, disease, and disintegration for many countries.

Table 1. **Declines in Total Fertility Rates: Selected Years**

Country	Year	Fertility level	Annual average fertility decline (Percent)
Hong Kong	1961	5,170	
	1971	3,423	4.0
Singapore	1960	5,078	
	1970	3,088	6.4
Taiwan	1960	5,750	
	1970	4,000	3.6
South Korea	1960	6,184	
	1970	3,937	4.4
West Malaysia	1960	5,955	
	1970	5,051	1.6
Sri Lanka	1960	5,496	
	1970	4,414	2.4
Barbados	1960	4,675	
	1970	2,705	5.3
Chile	1960	5,146	
	1970	3,653	3.4
Costa Rica	1960	7,355	
	1970	4,950	3.9
Trinidad & Tobago	1960	5,550	
	1970	3,387	4.8
Mauritius	1960	5,897	
	1970	3,387	5.4
Egypt	1960	6,381	
	1970	5,095	2.2
Fiji	1960	5603	
	1970	3,841	5.4

Source of basic data: ISPC, U.S. Bureau of the Census

Total Fertility Rate: Number of children a woman would have if she were to bear them at the prevailing rate in each five-year age group of woman's reproductive span (ages 15-19,20-24...45-49). Rates in this table refer to number of children per 1,000 women.

LIVE BIRTHS PER 1,000 POPULATION

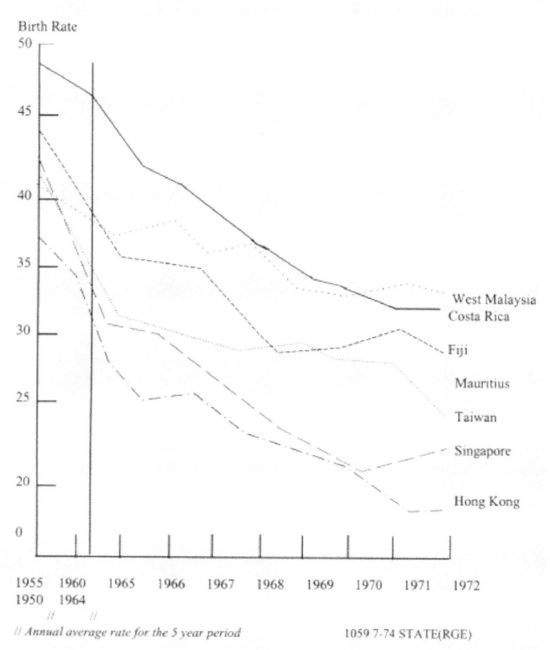

// Annual average rate for the 5 year period   1059 7-74 STATE(RGE)

Projection (c) is attainable if countries recognized the gravity of their population situation and By

Table 2. - World Population Growth Under Different
Assumptions Concerning Fertility: 1970-2075

	Constant Fertility Variant		Medium Fertility Variant		Replacement Fertility Variant	
	Millions	Growth*	Millions	Growth*	Millions	Growth*
1970	3,600	-	3,600	-	3,600	-
1985	5,200	2.4%	4,858	2.0%	4,783	1.8%
2000	7,800	2.8%	6,407	1.9%	5,923	1.4%
2075	103,000	3.4%	12,048	0.84%	8,357	0.46%

* Annual average growth rate since preceding date.

Furthermore, after replacement level fertility is reached, family size need not remain at an average of two children per family. Once this level is attained, it is possible that fertility will continue to decline below replacement level. This would hasten the time when a stationary population is reached and would increase the difference between the projection variants.

The great momentum of population growth can be seen even more clearly in the case of a single country -- for example, Mexico. Its 1970 population was 50 million. If its 1965-1970 fertility were to continue, Mexico's population in 2070 would theoretically number 2.2 billion. If its present average of 6.1 children per family could be reduced to an average of about 2 (replacement level fertility) by 1980-85, its population would continue to grow for about **sixty** years to 110 million. If the two-child average could be reached by 1990-95, the population would stabilize in sixty more years at about 22 percent higher -- 134 million. If the two-child average cannot be reached for 30 years (by 2000-05), the population at stabilization would grow by an additional 24 percent to 167 million.

Similar illustrations for other countries are given below.

Table 3.   Projected Population Size Under Different Assumptions Concerning
             Fertility: 1970-2070

to Country	Fertility assumption	Population in millions			Ratio of 2070 to 1970 population
		1970	2000	2070	
Venezuela	Constant fertility	11	31	420	38.2
	Replacement fertility by:				
	2000-05		22	34	3.1
	1990-95		20	27	2.4
	1980-85		18	22	2.0
Indonesia	Constant fertility	120	294	4,507	37.6
	Replacement fertility by:				
	2000-05		214	328	2.7
	1990-95		193	275	2.3
	1980-85		177	236	2.0
Morocco	Constant fertility	16	54	1,505	14.1
	Replacement fertility by:				
	2000-05		35	58	3.6
	1990-95		30	44	2.8
	1980-85		26	35	2.2

Source of basic data: ISPC, U.S. Bureau of the Census

As Table 3 indicates, alternative rates of fertility decline would have significant impact on the size of a country's population by 2000. They would make enormous differences in the sizes of the stabilized populations, attained some 60 to 70 years after replacement level fertility is reached. Therefore, it is of the utmost urgency that governments now recognize the facts and implications of population growth determining the ultimate population sizes that make sense for their countries and start vigorous programs at once to achieve their desired goals.

Future Growth in Major Regions and Countries

Throughout the projected period 1970 to 2000, less developed regions will grow more rapidly than developed regions. The rate of growth in LDCs will primarily depend upon the rapidity with which family planning practices are adopted..

Differences in the growth rates of DCs and LDCs will further aggravate the striking demographic imbalances between developed and less developed countries. Under the U.N. medium projection variant, by the year 2000 the population of less developed countries would double, rising from 2.5 billion in 1970 to 5.0 billion (Table 4). In contrast, the overall growth of the population of the developed world during the same period would amount to about 26 percent, increasing from 1.08 to 1.37 billion. Thus, by the year 2000 almost 80 percent of world population would reside in regions now considered less developed and over 90 percent of the annual increment to world population would occur there.

The paucity of reliable information on all Asian communist countries and the highly optimistic assumptions concerning China's fertility trends implicit in U.N. medium projections1/ argue for desegregating the less developed countries into centrally planned economies and countries with market economies. Such desegregation reflects more accurately the burden of rapidly growing populations in most LDCs.

As Table 4 shows, the population of countries with centrally planned economies, comprising about 1/3 of the 1970 LDC total, is projected to grow between 1970 and 2000 at a rate well below the LDC average of 2.3 percent. Over the entire thirty-year period, their growth rate averages 1.4 percent, in comparison with 2.7 percent for other LDCs. Between 1970 and 1985, the annual rate of growth in Asian communist LDCs is expected to average 1.6 percent and subsequently to decline to an average of 1.2 percent between 1985 and 2000. The growth rate of LDCs with market economies, on the other hand, remains practically the same, at 2.7 and 2.6 percent, respectively. Thus, barring both large-scale birth control efforts (greater than implied by the medium variant) or economic or political upheavals, the next twenty-five years offer non-communist LDCs little respite from the burdens of rapidly increasing humanity. Of course, some LDCs will be able to accommodate this increase with less difficulty than others.

Moreover, short of Draconian measures there is no possibility that any LDC can stabilize its population at less than double its present size. For many, stabilization will not tee short of three times their present size.

1/ The size of the Chinese population, its age distribution and rate of growth are widely disputed, not only among western observers but apparently within China itself. Recent estimates vary from "over 700   million," a figure used consistently by PR China's representatives to U.N. meetings, to 920 million   estimated for mid-1974 by U.S. Department of Commerce, Bureau of Economic Analysis.

TABLE 4. TOTAL POPULATION, DISTRIBUTION, AND
RATES OF GROWTH, by Major Region: 1970-2000

(UN "medium" projection variant)

Major Region and Country	Total Population					Growth	
	1970		1985	2000		1970-2000	
	Mil-lions	Per-cent	Mil-lions	Mil-lions	Per-cent	Mil-lions	Annual average
WORLD TOTAL	3,621	100.0	4,858	6,407	100.0	2,786	1.9%
DEVELOPED COUNTRIES	1,084	29.9	1,234	1,368	21.4	284	0.8%
Market economies	736	20.3	835	920	14.4	184	0.7%
US	205	5.7	236	264	4.1	59	0.9%
Japan	104	2.9	122	133	2.1	29	0.8%
Centrally planned economies	348	9.6	399	447	7.0	99	0.8%
USSR	243	6.7	283	321	5.0	78	0.9%
LESS DEVELOPED COUNTRIES	2,537	70.1	3,624	5,039	78.6	2,502	2.3%
Centrally planned economies*	794	21.9	1,007	1,201	18.7	407	1.4%
China	756	20.9	955	1,127	17.6	369	1.3%
Market economies	1,743	48.1	2,616	3,838	59.9	2,095	2.7%
East Asia	49	1.4	66	83	1.3	34	1.8%
South Asia	1,090	30.1	1,625	2,341	36.5	1,251	2.6%
Eastern South Asia	264	7.3	399	574	9.0	310	2.6%
Indonesia	120	3.3	177	250	3.9	130	2.5%
Middle South Asia	49	20.7	1,105	1,584	24.7	835	2.5%
Indian sub-continent**	691	19.1	1,016	1,449	22.6	758	2.5%
Western South Asia	77	2.1	121	183	2.9	106	2.9%
Africa	352	9.7	536	884	13.1	482	2.9%
Nigeria	55	1.5	84	135	2.1	80	3.0%
Egypt	33	0.9	47	66	1.0	33	2.3%
Latin America	248	6.8	384	572	8.9	324	2.8%
Caribbean	26	0.7	36	48	0.8	22	2.2%
Central America	67	1.8	109	173	2.7	106	3.2%
Mexico	50	1.4	83	132	2.1	82	3.3%
Tropical S. America	155	4.3	239	351	5.5	196	2.8%
Brazil	95	2.6	145	212	3.3	117	2.7%
Columbia	22	0.6	35	51	0.8	29	2.9%
Oceania	4	0.1	6	9	0.1	5	2.6%

* Centrally planned economies include PR-China, North Korea, North Vietnam and Mongolia.

NATO and Eastern Europe.   In the west, only France and Greece have a policy of increasing population growth -- which the people are successfully disregarding. (In a recent and significant change from traditional positions, however, the French Assembly overwhelmingly endorsed a law not only authorizing general availability of contraceptives but also providing that their cost be borne by the social security system.) Other western NATO members have no policies.1/ Most provide some or substantial family planning services. All appear headed toward lower growth rates. In two NATO member countries (West Germany and Luxembourg), annual numbers of deaths already exceed births, yielding a negative natural growth rate.

Romania, Hungary, Bulgaria, and Czechoslovakia have active policies to increase their population growth rates despite the reluctance of their people to have larger families. Within the USSR, fertility rates in RSFSR and the republics of Ukraine, Latvia, and Estonia are below replacement level. This situation has prevailed at least since 1969-1970 and, if continued, will eventually lead to negative population growth in these republics. In the United States, average fertility also fell below replacement level in the past two years (1972 and 1973). There is a striking difference, however, in the attitudes toward this demographic development in the two countries. While in the United States the possibility of a stabilized (non-growing) population is generally viewed with favor, in the USSR there is perceptible concern over the low fertility of Slavs and Balts (mostly by Slavs and Balts). The Soviet government, by all indications, is studying the feasibility of increasing their sagging birth rates. The entire matter of fertility-bolstering policies is circumscribed by the relatively high costs of increasing fertility (mainly through increased outlays for consumption goods and services) and the need to avoid the appearance of ethnic discrimination between rapidly and slowly growing nationalities.

U.N. medium projections to the year 2000 show no significant changes in the relative demographic position of the western alliance countries as against eastern Europe and the USSR. The population of the Warsaw Pact countries will remain at 65 percent of the populations of NATO member states. If Turkey is excluded, the Warsaw Pact proportion rises somewhat from 70 percent in 1970 to 73 percent by 2000. This change is not of an order of magnitude that in itself will have important implications for east-westpower relations. (Future growth of manpower in NATO and Warsaw Pact nations has not been examined in this Memorandum.)

Of greater potential political and strategic significance are prospective changes in the populations of less developed regions both among themselves and in relation to developed countries.

Africa.   Assessment of future demographic trends in Africa is severely impeded by lack of reliable base data on the size, composition, fertility and mortality, and migration of much of the continent's population. With this important limitation in mind, the population of Africa is projected to increase from 352 million in 1970 to 834 million in 2000, an increase of almost 2.5 times. In most African countries, population growth rates are likely to increase appreciably

---

1/ Turkey has a policy of population control.

before they begin to decline. Rapid population expansion may be particularly burdensome to the "least developed" among Africa's LDCs including according to the U.N. classification -- Ethiopia, Sudan, Tanzania, Uganda, Upper Volta, Mali, Malawi, Niger, Burundi, Guinea, Chad, Rwanda, Somalia, Dahomey, Lesotho, and Botswana. As a group, they numbered 104 million in 1970 and are projected to grow at an average rate of 3.0 percent a year, to some 250 million in 2000. This rate of growth is based on the assumption of significant reductions in mortality. It is questionable, however, whether economic and social conditions in the foreseeable future will permit reductions in mortality required to produce a 3 percent growth rate. Consequently, the population of the "least developed" of Africa's LDCs may fall short of the 250 million figure in 2000.

African countries endowed with rich oil and other natural resources may be in a better economic position to cope with population expansion. Nigeria falls into this category. Already the most populous country on the continent, with an estimated 55 million people in 1970 (see footnote to Table 4), Nigeria's population by the end of this century is projected to number 135 million. This suggests a growing political and strategic role for Nigeria, at least in Africa south of the Sahara.

In North Africa, Egypt's population of 33 million in 1970 is projected to double by 2000. The large and increasing size of Egypt's population is, and will remain for many years, an important consideration in the formulation of many foreign and domestic policies not only of Egypt but also of neighbouring countries.

Latin America. Rapid population growth is projected for tropical South American which includes Brazil, Colombia, Peru, Venezuela, Ecuador and Bolivia. Brazil, with a current population of over 100 million, clearly dominates the continent demographically; by the end of this century, its population is projected to reach the 1974 U.S. level of about 212 million people. Rapid economic grows] prospects -- if they are not diminished by demographic overgrowth -- portend a growing power status for Brazil in Latin America and on the world scene over the next 25 years.

The Caribbean which includes a number of countries with promising family planning programs Jamaica, Trinidad and Tobago, Cuba, Barbados and also Puerto Rico) is projected to grow a 2.2 percent a year between 1970 and 2000, a rate below the Latin American average of 2.8 percent.

Perhaps the most significant population trend from the view point of the United States is the prospect that Mexico's population will increase from 50 million in 1970 to over 130 million by the year 2000. Even under most optimistic conditions, in which the country's average fertility falls to replacement level by 2000, Mexico's population is likely to exceed 100 million by the end of this century.

South Asia. Somewhat slower rates are expected for Eastern and Middle South Asia whose combined population of 1.03 billion in 1970 is projected to more than double by 2000 to 2.20 billion. In the face of continued rapid population growth (2.5 percent), the prospects for the populous Indian subregion, which already faces staggering economic problems, are particularly bleak. South and Southeast Asia's population will substantially increase relative to mainland China; it appears doubtful, however, that this will do much to enhance their relative power position and political influence in Asia. On the contrary, preoccupation with the growing internal economic and social problems resulting from huge population increases may progressively reduce the ability of the region, especially India, to play an effective regional and world power role.

Western South Asia, demographically dominated by Turkey and seven oil-rich states (including Saudi Arabia, Iraq, and Kuwait) is projected to be one of the fastest growing LDC regions, with an annual average growth rate of 2.9 percent between 1970 and 2000. Part of this growth will be due to immigration, as for example, into Kuwait.

The relatively low growth rate of 1.8 percent projected for East Asian LDCs with market economics reflects highly successful family planning programs in Taiwan, South Korea, and Hong Kong.

The People's Republic of China (PRC).   The People's Republic of China has by far the world's largest population and, potentially, severe problems of population pressure, given its low standard of living and quite intensive utilization of available farm land resources. Its last census in 1953 recorded a population of 583 million, and PRC officials have cited a figure as high as 830 million for 1970. The Commerce Department's Bureau of Economic Analysis projects a slightly higher population, reaching 920 million by 1974. The present population growth rate is about two percent.

Conclusion

Rapid population growth in less developed countries has been mounting in a social milieu of poverty, unemployment and underemployment, low educational attainment, widespread malnutrition, and increasing costs of food production. These countries have accumulated a formidable "backlog" of unfinished tasks. They include economic assimilation of some 40 percent of their people who are pressing at, but largely remain outside the periphery of the developing economy; the amelioration of generally low levels of living; and in addition, accommodation of annually larger increments to the population. The accomplishment of these tasks could be intolerably slow if the average annual growth rate in the remainder of this century does not slow down to well below the 2.7 percent projected, under the medium variant, for LDCs with market economics. How rapid population growth impedes social and economic progress is discussed in subsequent chapters.

Projected Growth of Urban Population, Selected Years 1965-2000
(U.N. Medium Variant)

Year	World Population			DC Population			LDC Population		
	Total	Urban	Percent	Total	Urban	Percent	Total	Urban	Percent
	(millions)		urban	(millions)		urban	(millions)		urban
1965	3,289	1,158	35.2	1,037	651	62.8	2,252	507	22.5
1970	3,621	1,315	36.3	1,084	693	63.9	2,537	622	24.5
1980	4,401	1,791	40.7	1,183	830	70.2	3,218	961	29.9
1990	5,346	2,419	45.3	1,282	977	76.2	4,064	1,443	35.5
2000	6,407	3,205	50.0	1,368	1,118	81.8	5,039	2,087	41.4

Note: The 'urban' population has...... been estimated in accordance with diverse national definitions of that term.

Rates of Growth of Urban and Rural Populations, 1970-2000
(U.N. Medium Variant)

1970-2000	World Population			DC Population			LDC Population		
	Total	Urban	Rural	Total	Urban	Rural	Total	Urban	Rural
Total growth (percent)	76.9	143.7	38.8	26.2	61.3	-36.1	98.6	235.5	54.2
Annual average growth (percent)	1.9	3.0	1.1	0.8	1.6	- 1.5	2.3	4.1	1.5

CHAPTER II - POPULATION AND WORLD FOOD SUPPLIES

Rapid population growth and lagging food production in developing countries, together with the sharp deterioration in the global food situation in 1972 and 1973, have raised serious concerns about the ability of the world to feed itself adequately over the next quarter century and beyond.

As a result of population growth, and to some extent also of increasing affluence, world food demand has been growing at unprecedented rates. In 1900, the annual increase in world demand for cereals was about 4 million tons. By 1950, it had risen to about 12 million tons per year. By 1970, the annual increase in demand was 30 million tons (on a base of over 1,200 million tons). This is roughly equivalent to the annual wheat crop of Canada, Australia, and Argentina combined. This annual increase in food demand is made up of a 2 % annual increase in population and a 0.5 % increased demand per capita. Part of the rising per capita demand reflects improvement in diets of some of the peoples of the developing countries. In the less developed countries about 400 pounds of grain is available per person per year and is mostly eaten as cereal. The average North American, however, uses nearly a ton of grain a year, only 200 pounds directly and the rest in the form of meat, milk, and eggs for which several pounds of cereal are required to produce one pound of the animal product (e.g., five pounds of grain to produce one pound of beef).

During the past two decades, LDCs have been able to keep food production ahead of population, notwithstanding the unprecedent- edly high rates of population growth. The basic figures are summarized in the following table: [calculated from data in USDA, The World Agricultural Situation, March 1974]:

INDICES OF WORLD POPULATION AND FOOD PRODUCTION
(excluding Peoples Republic of China)
1954=100

	WORLD			DEVELOPED COUNTRIES			LESS DEVELOPED COUNTRIES		
	Food Production			Food Production			Food production		
	Population	Total	Per Capital	Population	Total	Per Capital	Population	Total	Per Cap.
1954	100	100	100	100	100	100	100	100	100
1973	144	170	119	124	170	138	159	171	107
Compound Annual increase (%)	1.9	2.8	0.9	1.1	2.8	1.7	2.5	0 2.9	0.4

It will be noted that the relative gain in LDC total food production was just as great as for advanced countries, but was far less on a per capita basis because of the sharp difference in population growth rates. Moreover, within the LDC group were 24 countries (including Indonesia, Nigeria, the Philippines, Zaire, Algeria, Guyana, Iraq, and Chile) in which the rate of increase of population growth exceeded the rate of increase in food production; and a much more populous group (including India, Pakistan, and Bangladesh) in which the rate of increase in production barely exceeded population growth but did not keep up with the increase in domestic demand. [World Food Conference, Preliminary Assessment, 8 May 1974; U.N. Document E/CONF. 65/PREP/6, p. 33.]

General requirements have been projected for the years 1985 and 2000, based on the UN Medium Variant population estimates and allowing for a very small improvement in diets in the LDCs.

A recent projection made by the Department of Agriculture indicates a potential productive capacity more than adequate to meet world cereal requirements (the staple food of the world) of a population of 6.4 billion in the year 2000 (medium fertility variant) at roughly current relative prices.

This overall picture offers little cause for complacency when broken down by geographic regions. To support only a very modest improvement in current cereal consumption levels (from 177 kilograms per capita in 1970 to 200-206 kilograms in 2000) the projections show an alarming increase in LDC dependency on imports. Such imports are projected to rise from 21.4 million tons in 1970 to 102-122 million tons by the end of the century. Cereal imports would increase to 13-15 percent of total developing country consumption as against 8 percent in 1970. As a group, the advanced countries cannot only meet their own needs but will also generate a substantial surplus. For the LDCs, analyses of food production capacity foresee the physical possibility of meeting their needs, provided that (a) weather conditions are normal, (b) yields per unit of area continue to improve at the rates of the last decade, bringing the average by 1985 close to present yields in the advanced countries, and (c) a substantially larger annual transfer of grains can be arranged from the surplus countries (mainly North America), either through commercial sales or through continuous and growing food aid. The estimates of production capacity do not rely on major new technical breakthroughs in food production methods, but they do require the availability and application of greatly increased quantities of fertilizers, pesticides, irrigation water, and other inputs to modernized agriculture, together with continued technological advances at past rates and the institutional and administrative reforms (including vastly expanded research and extension services) essential to the successful application of these inputs. They also assume normal weather conditions. Substantial political will is required in the LDCs to give the necessary priority to food production.

There is great uncertainty whether the conditions for achieving food balance in the LDCs can in fact be realized. Climatic changes are poorly understood, but a persistent atmospheric cooling trend since 1940 has been established. One respectable body of scientific opinion believes that this portends a period of much wider annual frosts, and possibly a long-term lowering of rainfall in the monsoon areas of Asia and Africa. Nitrogen fertilizer will be in world short supply into the late 1970s, at least; because of higher energy prices, it may also be more costly in real terms than in the 1960s. Capital investments for irrigation and infrastructure and the organizational requirements for securing continuous improvements in agricultural yields may well be beyond the financial and administrative capacity of many LDCs. For some of the areas under heaviest population pressure, there is little or no prospect for foreign exchange earnings to cover constantly increasing imports of food.

While it is always unwise to project the recent past into the long-term future, the experience of 1972-73 is very sobering. The coincidence of adverse weather in many regions in 1972 brought per capita production in the LDCs back to the level of the early 1960s. At the same time, world food reserves (mainly American) were almost exhausted, and they were not rebuilt during the high production year of 1973. A repetition under these conditions of 1972 weather patterns would result in large-scale famine of a kind not experienced for several decades -- a kind the world thought had been permanently banished.

Even if massive famine can be averted, the most optimistic forecasts of food production potential in the more populous LDCs show little improvement in the presently inadequate levels and quality of nutrition. As long as annual population growth continues at 2 to 3 percent or more,

LDCs must make expanded food production the top development priority, even though it may absorb a large fraction of available capital and foreign exchange.

Moderation of population growth rates in the LDCs could make some difference to food requirements by 1985, a substantial difference by 2000, and a vast difference in the early part of the next century. From the viewpoint of U.S. interests, such reductions in LDC food needs would be clearly advantageous. They would not reduce American commercial markets for food since the reduction in LDC food requirements that would result from slowing population growth would affect only requests for concessional or grant food assistance, not commercial sales. They would improve the prospects for maintaining adequate world food reserves against climatic emergencies. They would reduce the likelihood of periodic famines in region after region, accompanied by food riots and chronic social and political instability. They would improve the possibilities for long-term development and integration into a peaceful world order.

Even taking the most optimistic view of the theoretical possibilities of producing enough foods in the developed countries to meet the requirements of the developing countries, the problem of increased costs to the LDCs is already extremely serious and in its future may be insurmountable. At current prices the anticipated import requirements of 102-122 million tons by 2000 would raise the cost of developing countries' imports of cereals to $16-20 1/ billion by that year compared with $2.5 billion in 1970. Large as they may seem even these estimates of import requirements could be on the low side if the developing countries are unable to achieve the Department of Agriculture's assumed increase in the rate of growth of production.

The FAO in its recent "Preliminary Assessment of the World Food Situation Present and Future" has reached a similar conclusion:

> What is certain is the enormity of the food import bill which might face the developing countries . . . In addition [to cereals] the developing countries . . . would be importing substantial amounts of other foodstuffs. clearly the financing of international food trade on this scale would raise very grave problems.

At least three-quarters of the projected increase in cereal imports of developing countries would fall in the poorer countries of South Asia and North and Central Africa. The situation in Latin America which is projected to shift from a modest surplus to a modest deficit area is quite different. Most of this deficit will be in Mexico and Central America, with relatively high income and easily exploitable transportation links to the U.S.

The problem in Latin America, therefore, appears relatively more manageable.

It seems highly unlikely, however, that the poorer countries of Asia and Africa will be

---

1/ At $160.00 per ton.

able to finance nearly like the level of import requirements projected by the USDA. Few of them have dynamic export-oriented industrial sectors like Taiwan or South Korea or rich raw material resources that will generate export earnings fast enough to keep pace with food import needs. Accordingly, those countries where large-scale hunger and malnutrition are already present face the bleak prospect of little, if any, improvement in the food intake in the years ahead barring a major foreign financial food aid program, more rapid expansion of domestic food production, reduced population growth or some combination of all three. Worse yet, a series of crop disasters could transform some of them into classic Malthusian cases with famines involving millions of people.

While foreign assistance probably will continue to be forthcoming to meet short-term emergency situations like the threat of mass starvation, it is more questionable whether aid donor countries will be prepared to provide the sort of massive food aid called for by the import projections on a long-term continuing basis.

Reduced population growth rates clearly could bring significant relief over the longer term. Some analysts maintain that for the post-1985 period a rapid decline in fertility will be crucial to adequate diets worldwide. If, as noted before, fertility in the developing countries could be made to decline to the replacement level by the year 2000, the world's population in that year would be 5.9 billion or 500 million below the level that would be attained if the UN medium projection were followed. Nearly all of the decline would be in the LDCs. With such a reduction the projected import gap of 102-122 million tons per year could be eliminated while still permitting a modest improvement in per capita consumption. While such a rapid reduction in fertility rates in the next 30 years is an optimistic target, it is thought by some experts that it could be obtained by intensified efforts if its necessity were understood by world and national leaders. Even more modest reductions could have significant implications by 2000 and even more over time.

Intensive programs to increase food production in developing countries beyond the levels assumed in the U.S.D.A. projections probably offer the best prospect for some reasonably early relief, although this poses major technical and organizational difficulties and will involve substantial costs. It must be realized, however, that this will be difficult in all countries and probably impossible in some — or many. Even with the introduction of new inputs and techniques it has not been possible to increase agricultural output by as much as 3 percent per annum in many of the poorer developing countries. Population growth in a number of these countries exceeds that rate.

Such a program of increased food production would require the widespread use of improved seed varieties, increased applications of chemical fertilizers and pesticides over vast areas and better farm management along with bringing new land under cultivation. It has been estimated, for example, that with better varieties, pest control, and the application of fertilizer on the Japanese scale, Indian rice yields could theoretically at least, be raised two and one-half times current levels. Here again very substantial foreign assistance for imported materials may be required for at least the early years before the program begins to take hold.

The problem is clear. The solutions, or at least the directions we must travel to reach them are also generally agreed. <u>What will be required</u> is a genuine commitment to a set of policies that will lead the international community, both developed and developing countries, to the achievement of the objectives spelled out above.

CHAPTER III - <u>MINERALS AND FUEL</u>

Population growth per se is not likely to impose serious constraints on the global physical availability of fuel and non-fuel minerals to the end of the century and beyond.

This favourable outlook on reserves does not rule out shortage situations for specific minerals at particular times and places. Careful planning with continued scientific and technological progress (including the development of substitutes) should keep the problems of physical availability within manageable proportions.

The major factor influencing the demand for non-agricultural raw materials is the level of industrial activity, regional and global. For example, the U.S., with 6% of the world's population, consumes about a third of its resources. The demand for raw 0materials, unlike food, is not a direct function of population growth. The current scarcities and high prices for most such materials result mainly from the boom conditions in all industrialized regions in the years 1972-73.

The important potential linkage between rapid population growth and minerals availability is indirect rather than direct. It flows from the negative effects of excessive population growth in economic development and social progress, and therefore on internal stability, in overcrowded under-developed countries. The United States has become increasingly dependent on mineral imports from developing countries in recent decades, and this trend is likely to continue.   The location of known reserves of higher-grade ores of most minerals favours increasing dependence of all industrialized regions on imports from less developed countries. The real problems of mineral supplies lie, not in basic physical sufficiency, but in the politico-economic issues of access, terms for exploration and exploitation, and division of the benefits among producers, consumers, and host country governments.

In the extreme cases where population pressures lead to endemic famine, food riot, and breakdown of social order, those conditions are scarcely conducive to systematic exploration for mineral deposits or the long-term investments required for their exploitation. Short of famine, unless some minimum of popular aspirations for material improvement can be satisfied, and unless the terms of access and exploitation persuade governments and peoples that this aspect of the international economic order has "something in it for them," concessions to foreign companies are likely to be expropriated or subjected to arbitrary intervention.   Whether through government action, labor conflicts, sabotage, or civil disturbance, the smooth flow of needed Materials will be jeopardized. Although population pressure is obviously not the only factor involved, these types of frustrations are much less likely under conditions of slow or zero population growth.

<u>Reserves</u>

Projections made by the Department of Interior through the year 2000 for those fuel and non-fuel minerals on which the U.S. depends heavily for imports1/ support these conclusions on physical resources (see Annex). Proven reserves of many of these minerals appear to be more than adequate to meet the estimated accumulated world demand at 1972 relative prices at least to the end of the century. While petroleum (including natural gas), copper, zinc, and tin are probable exceptions, the extension of economically exploitable reserves as a result of higher prices, as well as substitution and secondary recovery for metals, should avoid long-term supply restrictions. In many cases, the price increases that have taken place since 1972 should be more than sufficient to bring about the necessary extension of reserves.

These conclusions are consistent with a much more extensive study made in 1972 for the Commission on Population Growth and the American Future.2/

As regards fossil fuels, that study foresees adequate world reserves for at least the next quarter to half century even without major technological breakthroughs. U.S. reserves of coal and oil shale are adequate well into the next century, although their full exploitation may be limited by environmental and water supply factors. Estimates of the U.S. Geological Survey suggest recoverable oil and gas reserves (assuming sufficiently high prices) to meet domestic demand for another two or three decades, but there is also respectable expert opinion supporting much lower estimates; present oil production is below the peak of 1970 and meets only 70 percent of current demands.3/ Nevertheless, the U.S. is in a relatively strong position on fossil fuels compared with the rest of the industrialized world, provided that it takes the time and makes the heavy investments needed to develop domestic alternatives to foreign sources.

In the case of the 197 non-fuel minerals studied by the Commission it was concluded there were sufficient proven reserves of nine to meet cumulative world needs at current relative prices through the year 2020.4/ For the ten others5/ world proven reserves were considered inadequate. However, it was judged that moderate price increases, recycling and substitution could bridge the estimated gap between supply and requirements.

The above projections probably understate the estimates of global resources. "Proved Reserves," that is known supplies that will be available at present or slightly higher relative costs 10 to 25 years from now, rarely exceed 25 years' cumulative requirements, because industry generally is reluctant to undertake costly exploration to meet demands which may or may not materialize in the more distant future. Experience has shown that additional reserves are discovered as required, at least in the case of non-fuel minerals, ant "proved reserves" have generally remained constant in relation to consumption.

1/ Aluminum, copper, iron ore, lead, nickel, tin, uranium, zinc, and petroleum (including natural gas).
2/ Population, Resources and the Environment, edited by Ronald Ridker, Vol. III of the Commission Research Report
3/ For a recent review of varying estimates on oil and gas reserves, see Oil and Gas Resources, Science, , 12 July 74, pp. 127-130 (Vol. 185).
4/ Chromium, iron, nickel, vanadium, magnesium, phosphorous, potassium, cobalt, and nitrogen.
5/ Manganese, molybdenum, tungsten, aluminum, copper, lead, zinc, tin, titanium, and sulphur.

The adequacy of reserves does not of course assure that supplies will be forthcoming in a steady stream as required. Intermediate problems may develop as a result of business miscalculations regarding the timing of expansion to meet requirements. With the considerable lead time required for expanding capacity, this can result in periods of serious shortage for certain materials and rising prices as in the recent past. Similarly, from time to time there will be periods of overcapacity and falling prices. Necessary technical adjustments required for the shift to substitutes or increased recycling also may be delayed by the required lead time or by lack of information.

An early warning system designed to flag impending surpluses and shortages, could be very helpful in anticipating these problems. Such a mechanism might take the form of groups of experts working with the UN Division of Resources. Alternatively, intergovernmental commodity study groups might be set up for the purpose of monitoring those commodities identified as potential problem areas.

Adequate global availability of fuel and non-fuel minerals is not of much benefit to countries who cannot afford to pay for them. Oil supplies currently are adequate to cover world needs, but the quadrupling of prices in the past year has created grave financial and payment problems for developed and developing countries alike. If similar action to raise prices were undertaken by supplies of other important minerals, an already bad situation would be intensified. Success in such efforts is questionable, however; there is no case in which the quantities involved are remotely comparable to the cases of energy; and the scope for successful price-gouging or cartel tactics is much smaller.

Although the U.S. is relatively well off in this regard, it nonetheless depends heavily on mineral imports from a number of sources which are not completely safe or stable. It may therefore be necessary, especially in the light of our recent oil experience, to keep this dependence within bounds, in some cases by developing additional domestic resources and more generally by acquiring stockpiles for economic as well as national defence emergencies. There are also possible dangers of unreasonable prices promoted by producer cartels and broader policy questions of U.S. support for commodity agreements involving both producers and consumers. Such matters, however, are in the domain of commodity policy rather than population policy.

At least through the end of this century, changes in population growth trends will make little difference to total levels of requirements for fuel and other minerals. Those requirements are related much more closely to levels of income and industrial output, leaving the demand for minerals substantially unaffected. In the longer run, a lower ultimate world population (say 8 to 9 billion rather than 12 to 16 billion) would require a lower annual input of depletable resources directly affected by population size as well as a much lower volume of food, forest products, textiles, and other renewable resources.

Whatever may be done to guard against interruptions of supply and to develop domestic alternatives, the U.S. economy will require large and increasing amounts of minerals from abroad, especially from less developed countries.7/ That fact gives the U.S. enhanced interest in the political, economic, and social stability of the supplying countries. Wherever a lessening of population pressures through reduced birth rates can increase the prospects for such stability, population policy becomes relevant to resource supplies and to the economic interests of the United States.

7/ See National Commission on Materials Policy, Towards a National Materials Policy: Basic Data and Issues, April 1972].

ANNEX

OUTLOOK FOR RAW MATERIALS

I.   Factors Affecting Raw Material Demand and Supply

Some of the key factors that must be considered in evaluating the future raw materials situation are the stage of a country's economic development and the responsiveness of the market to changes in the relative prices of the raw materials.

Economic theory indicates that the pattern of consumption of raw materials varies with the level of economic activity. Examination of the intensity-of- use of raw materials (incremental quantity of raw material needed to support an additional unit of GNP) show that after a particular level of GNP is reached, the intensity of use of raw materials starts to decline. Possible explanations for this decline are:

1.   In industrialized countries, the services component of GNP expands relative to the non-services components as economic growth occurs.

2.   Technological progress, on the whole, tends to lower the intensity-of- use through greater efficiency in the use of raw materials-and development of alloys.

3.   Economic growth continues to be characterized by substitution of one material by another and substitution of synthetics for natural materials.8/

Most developed countries have reached this point of declining intensity-of- use.9/ For other countries that have not reached this stage of economic development, their population usually goes through a stage of rapid growth prior to industrialization. This is due to the relative ease in the application of improved health care policies and the resulting decline in their death rates, while birth rates remain high. Then the country's economy does begin to industrialize and grow more rapidly, the initial rapid rise in industrial production results in an increasing intensity-of-use of raw materials, until industrial production reached the level where the intensity- of-use begins to decline.

As was discussed above, changes in the relative prices of raw materials change the amount of economically recoverable reserves. Thus, the relative price level, smoothness of the

---

8/ Materials Requirements Abroad in the Year 2000, research project prepared for National Commission on Materials Policy by the Wharton School, University of Pennsylvania; pp. 9-10.
9/ United Nations symposium on Population; Resources, and Environment Stockholm, 9/26-10/5/73, E/Conf.6/CEP/3, p. 35.

adjustment process, and availability of capital for needed investment can also be expected to significantly influence raw materials' market conditions In addition, technological improvement in mining and metallurgy permits lower grade ores to be exploited without corresponding increases in costs.

The following table presents the 1972 net imports and the ratio of imports to total demand for nine commodities. The net import of these nine commodities represented 99 percent of the total trade deficit in minerals.

Commodity	1972 Net Imports ($Millions)**	Ratio of Imports to Total Demand
Aluminum	483.8	.286
Copper	206.4	.160
Iron	424.5	.049
Lead	102.9	.239
Nickel	477.1	.704
Tin	220.2	.943
Titanium	256.5	.469
Zinc	294.8	.517
Petroleum (including natural gas)	5,494.5	.246

The primary sources of these US imports during the period 1969-1972 were:

Commodity	Source & %
Aluminum	- Canada 76%
Copper	- Canada 31%, Peru 27%, Chile 22%
Iron	- Canada 50%, Venezuela 31 %
Lead	- Canada 29%, Peru 21%, Australia 21%
Nickel	- Canada 82%, Norway 8%
Tin	- Malaysia 64%, Thailand 27%
Titanium	- Japan 73%, USSR 19%
Zinc (Ore)	- Canada 60%, Mexico 24%
Zinc (Metal)	- Canada 48%, Australia 10%
Petroleum (crude)	- Canada 42%
Petroleum (crude)	-Venezuela 17%

---

* The values are based on U.S. 1972 prices for materials in primary form, and in some cases do not represent commercial value of the crude material. Source: Bureau of Mines.

II. World Reserves

The following table shows estimates of the world reserve position for these commodities. As mentioned earlier, the quantity of economically recoverable reserves increases with higher prices The following tables, based on Bureau of Mines information, provide estimates of reserves at various prices. (All prices are in constant 1972 dollars.)

Aluminum (Bauxite)

Price (per pound primary aluminum)

	Price A	Price B	Price C	Price D
	.23	.29	.33	.36
Reserves	(billion short tons, aluminum content)			
World	3.58	3.76	4.15	5.21
U.S.	.01	.02	.04	.09

Copper

	Price A	Price B	Price C	Price D
Price	(per pound refined copper)			
	.51	.60	.75	
Reserves	(million short tons)			
World	370	418	507	
U.S.	83	93	115	

Gold

Price (per troy ounce)

	58.60	90	100	150
Reserves	(million troy ounce)			
World	1,000	1,221	1,588	1,850
U.S.	82	120	200	240

Iron

Price (per short ton of primary iron contained in ore)

	17.80	20.80	23.80
Reserves	(billion short tons iron content)		
World	96.7	129.0	206.0
U.S.	2.0	2.7	18.0

	Price A	Price B	Price C	Price D

Lead

	Price (per pound primary lead metal)			
	.15	.18	.20	
Reserves	(million short tons, lead content)			
World	96.0	129.0	144.0	
U.S.	36.0	51.0	56.0	

Nickel

	Price (per pound of primary metal)			
	1.53	1.75	2.00	2.25
Reserves	(millions short tons)			
World	46.2	60.5	78.0	99.5
U.S.	.2	.2	.5	.5

Tin

	Price (per pound primary tin metal)			
	1.77	2.0	2.5	3.00
Reserves	(thousands of long tons - tin content)			

World	4,180	5,500	7,530	9,290
U.S.	5	9	100	200

Titanium

Price (per pound titanium in pigment)

	.45	.55	.60

Reserves (thousands short tons titanium content)

World	158,100	222,000	327,000
U.S.	32,400	45,000	60,000

Zinc

Price (per pound, prime western zinc delivered)

	.18	.25	.30

Reserves (million short tons, zinc content)

World	131	193	260
U.S.	30	40	50

Petroleum

Data necessary to quantify reserve-price relationships are not available. For planning purposes, however, Bureau of Mines use the rough assumption that a 100% increase in price would increase reserves by 10%. The average 1972 U.S. price was $3.39/bbl. with proven world reserves of 666.9 billion bbls. and U.S. reserves of 36.. billion barrels. Using the Bureau of Mines assumption, therefore,; doubling in world price (a U.S. price of $6.78/bbl.) would imply world reserves of 733.5 billion bbls. and U.S. reserves of 39.9 billion barrels.

Natural Gas

Price (wellhead price per thousand cubic feet)

	.186	.34	.44	.55

Reserves (trillion cubic feet)

World	1,156	6,130	10,240	15,599
U.S.	266	580	900	2,349

It should be noted that these statistics represent a shift in 1972 relative prices and assume constant 1972 technology. The development of new technology or a more dramatic shift in relative prices can have a significant impact on the supply of economically recoverable reserves. Aluminum is a case in point. It is the most abundant metallic element in the earth's crust and the supply of this resource is almost entirely determined by the price. Current demand and technology limit economically recoverable reserves to bauxite sources. Alternate sources of aluminum exist (e.g., alunite) and if improved technology is developed making these alternate sources commercially viable, supply constraints will not likely be encountered.

The above estimated reserve figures, while representing approximate orders of magnitude, are adequate to meet projected accumulated world demand (also very rough orders of magnitude) through the year 2000. In some cases, modest price increases above the 1972 level may be required to attract the necessary capital investment.

CHAPTER IV - Economic Development and Population Growth

Rapid population growth adversely affects every aspect of economic and social progress in developing countries. It absorbs large amounts of resources needed for more productive investment in development. It requires greater expenditures for health, education and other social services, particularly in urban areas. It increases the dependency load per worker so that a high fraction of the output of the productive age group is needed to support dependents. It reduces family savings and domestic investment. It increases existing severe pressures on limited agricultural land in countries where the world's "poverty problem" is concentrated. It creates a need for use of large amounts of scarce foreign exchange for food imports (or the loss of food surpluses for export). Finally, it intensifies the already severe unemployment and underemployment problems of many developing countries where not enough productive jobs are created to absorb the annual increments to the labor force.

Even in countries with good resource/population ratios, rapid population growth causes problems for several reasons: First, large capital investments generally are required to exploit unused resources. Second, some countries already have high and growing unemployment and lack the means to train new entrants to their labor force. Third, there are long delays between starting effective family planning programs and reducing fertility, and even longer delays between reductions in fertility and population stabilization. Hence there is substantial danger of vastly overshooting population targets if population growth is not moderated in the near future.

During the past decade, the developing countries have raised their GNP at a rate of 5 percent per annum as against 4.8 percent in developed countries. But at the same time the LDCs experienced an average annual population growth rate of 2.5 percent. Thus their per capita income growth rate was only 2.5 percent and in some of the more highly populated areas the increase in per capita incomes was less than 2 percent. This stands in stark contrast to 3.6 percent in the rich countries. Moreover, the low rate means that there' very little change in those countries whose per capita incomes $200 or less per annum. The problem has been further exacerbated in recent months by the dramatic increases in oil and fertilizer prices. The World Bank has estimated that the incomes of the million inhabitants of the countries hardest hit by the oil crisis will grow at less than 1% per capita per year of the remainder of the 1970s. Taking account of inequalities in income distribution, there will be well over 500 million people, with average incomes of less than $100 per capita, who will experience either no growth or negative growth in that period.

Moderation of population growth offers benefits in terms of resources saved for investment and/or higher per capita consumption. If resource requirements to support fewer children are reduced and the funds now allocated for construction of schools, houses, hospitals and other essential facilities are invested in productive activities, the impact on the growth of GNP and per capita income may be significant. In addition, economic and social progress resulting from population control will further contribute to the decline in fertility rates. The relationship is reciprocal, and can take the form of either a vicious or a virtuous circle.

This raises the question of how much more efficient expenditures for population control might be than in raising production through direct investments in additional irrigation and power projects and factories. While most economists today do not agree with the assumptions that went into early overly optimistic estimates of returns to population expenditures, there is general agreement that up to the point when cost per acceptor rises rapidly, family planning expenditures are generally considered the best investment a country can make in its own future.

II   Impact of Population Growth on Economic Development

In most, if not all, developing countries high fertility rates impose substantial economic costs and restrain economic growth. The main adverse macroeconomic effects may be analyzed in three general categories: (1) the saving effect, (2) "child quality" versus "child quantity", and (3) "capital deepening" versus "capital widening." These three categories are not mutually exclusive, but they highlight different familial and social perspectives. In addition, there are often longer-run adverse effects on agricultural output and the balance of payments.

(1) The saving effect. A high fertility economy has perforce a larger "burden of dependency" than a low fertility economy, because a larger proportion of the population consists of children too young to work. There are more non-working people to feed, house and rear, and there is a smaller surplus above minimum consumption available for savings and investment. It follows that a lower fertility rate can free resources from consumption; if saved and invested, these resources could contribute to economic growth. (There is much controversy on this; empirical studies of the savings effect have produced varying results.)

(2) Child quality versus quantity. Parents make investment decisions, in a sense, about their children. Healthier and better-educated children tend to be economically more productive, both as children and later as adults. In addition to the more-or-less conscious trade- offs parents can make about more education and better health per child, there are certain biologic adverse effects suffered by high birth order children such as higher mortality and limited brain growth due to higher incidence of malnutrition. It must be emphasized, however, that discussion of trade-offs between child quality and child quantity will probably remain academic with regard to countries where child mortality remains high. When parents cannot expect most children to survive to old age, they probably will continue to "over-compensate", using high fertility as a form of hedge to insure that they will have <u>some</u> living offspring able to support the parents in the distant future.

(3) Capital deepening versus widening. From the family's viewpoint high fertility is likely to reduce welfare per child; for the economy one may view high fertility as too rapid a growth in labor force relative to capital stock. Society's capital stock includes facilities such as schools and other educational inputs in addition to capital investments that raise workers' outputs in agriculture and manufacturing. For any given rate of capital accumulation, a lower population growth rate can help increase the amount of capital and education per worker, helping thereby to increase output and income per capita. The problem of migration to cities and the derived demand for urban infrastructure can also be analysed as problems of capital widening, which

draw resources away from growth-generating investments.

In a number of the more populous countries a fourth aspect rapid growth in numbers has emerged in recent years which 1: profound long-run consequences. Agricultural output was able keep pace or exceed population growth over the many decades population rise prior to the middle of this century, primer through steady expansion of acreage under cultivation. More recently, only marginal unused land has been available in India, Thailand, Java, Bangladesh, and other areas. As a result (a) la holdings have declined in size, and (b) land shortage has led deforestation and overgrazing, with consequent soil erosion and severe water pollution and increased urban migration. Areas that once earned foreign exchange through the export of food surpluses are now in deficit or face early transition to dependence on food imports. Although the scope for raising agricultural productivity is very great in many of these areas, the available technologies for doing so require much higher capital costs per acre and much larger foreign exchange outlays for "modern" inputs (chemical fertilizer, pesticides, petroleum fuels, etc.) than was the case with the traditional technologies. Thus the population growth problem can seen as an important long-run, or structural, contributor to current LDC balance of payments problems and to deterioration of the basic ecological infrastructure.

Finally, high fertility appears to exacerbate the maldistribution of income which is a fundamental economic and social problem in much of the developing world. Higher income families tend to have fewer children, spend more on the health and education of the children, have more wealth to pass on to these children in contrast to the several disadvantages that face the children of the poor. The latter tend to be more numerous, receiving less of an investment per child in their "human capital", leaving the children with economic, educational and social constraints similar to those which restrict the opportunities of the parents. In short, high fertility contributes to the intergenerational continuity of maldistributions of income an related social and political problems.

III.   The Effect of Development on Population Growth

The determinants of population growth are not well understood, especially for low income societies. Historical data show that declining fertility in Europe and North America has been associated with declining mortality and increasing urbanization, and generally with "modernization". Fertility declined substantially in the West without the benefit of sophisticated contraceptives. This movement from high fertility and high mortality to low fertility and low mortality is known as the "demographic transition". In many low income countries mortality has declined markedly since World War II (in large part form reduction in epidemic illness and famine), but fertility has remained high. Apart from a few pockets of low fertility in East Asia and the Caribbean, a significant demographic transition has not occurred in the third world. (The Chinese, however, make remarkable claims about their success in reducing birth rates, and qualified observers are persuaded that they have had unusual success even though specific demographic information is lacking.)

There is considerable, incontestable evidence in many developing countries that a larger (though not fully known) number of couples would like to have fewer children than possible generally here -- and that there is a large unsatisfied demand by these couples for family planning services. It is also now widely believed that something more that family planning services will be needed to motivate other couples to want smaller families and all couples to want replacement levels essential to the progress and growth of their countries.

There is also evidence, although it is not conclusive, that certain aspects of economic development and modernization are more directly related to lowered birth rates than others, and that selective developmental policies may bring about a demographic transition at substantially lower per capita income levels than in Europe, North America, and Japan.1/ Such selective policies would focus on improved health care and nutrition directed toward reduced infant and child mortality; universal schooling and adult literacy, especially for women; increasing the legal age of marriage; greater opportunities for female employment in the money economy; improved old-age social security arrangements; and agricultural modernization focussed on small farmers.

It is important that this focus be made in development programs because, given today's high population densities, high birth rates, and low income levels in much of Asia, Africa, and Latin America, if the demographic transition has to await overall development and modernization, the vicious circle of poverty, people, and unemployment may never be broken.

The causes of high birth rates in low income societies are generally explained in terms of three factors.

a.   Inadequacy of information and means. Actual family size in many societies is higher than desired family size owing to ignorance of acceptable birth control methods or unavailability of birth control devices and services. The importance of this factor is evidenced by many sociological investigations on "desired family size" versus actual size, by the substantial rates of acceptance for contraceptives when systematic family planning services are introduced. This factor has been a basic assumption in the family planning programs of official bilateral and multilateral programs in many countries over the past decade. Whatever the actual weight of this factor, which clearly varies from country to country and which shifts with changes in economic and social conditions, there remains without question a significant demand for family planning services.

b.   Inadequacy of motivation for reduced numbers of children. Especially in the rural areas of underdeveloped countries, which account for the major share of today's population growth, parents often want large numbers of children (especially boys) (i) to ensure that some will survive against the odds of high child mortality, (ii) to provide support for the parents in their old age, and (iii) to provide low cost farm labor. While these elements are present among rural populace, continued urbanization may reduce the need for sons in the longer term. The

---

1/ See James E. Kocher, Rural Development, Income Distribution, and Fertility Decline (Population Council, New York, 1973), and William Rich, smaller Families through Social and Economic Progress (Overseas Development Council, Wash., 1973).

absence of educational and employment opportunities for young women intensifies these same motivations by encouraging early marriage and early and frequent maternity. This factor suggests the crucial importance of selective development policies as a means of accelerating the reduction of fertility.

      c.   The "time lag". Family preferences and social institutions that favour high fertility change slowly. Even though mortality and economic conditions have improved significantly since World War II in LDCs, family expectations, social norms, and parental practice are slow to respond to these altered conditions. This factor leads to the need for large scale programs of information, education, and persuasion directed at lower fertility.

The three elements are undoubtedly intermixed in varying proportions in all underdeveloped countries with high birth rates. In most LDCs, many couples would reduce their completed family size if appropriate birth control methods were more easily available. The extent of this reduction, however, may still leave their completed family size at higher than mere replacement levels -- i.e., at levels implying continued but less rapid population growth. Many other couples would not reduce their desired family size merely if better contraceptives were available, either because they see large families as economically beneficial, or because of cultural factors, or because they misread their own economic interests.

Therefore, family planning supply (contraceptive technology and delivery systems) and demand (the motivation for reduced fertility) would not be viewed as mutually exclusive alternatives; they are complementary and may be mutually reinforcing. The selected point of focus mentioned earlier -- old age security pro-grams, maternal and child health programs, increased female education, increasing the legal age of marriage, financial incentives to "acceptors", personnel, -- are important, yet better information is required as to which measures are most cost-effective and feasible in a given situation and how their cost-effectiveness compares to supply programs.

One additional interesting area is receiving increasing attention: the distribution of the benefits of development. Experience in several countries suggests that the extent to which the poor, with the highest fertility rates, reduce their fertility will depend on the extent to which they participate in development. In this view the average level of economic development and the average amount of modernization are less important determinants of population growth than is the specific structure of development. This line of investigation suggests that social development activities need to be more precisely targeted than in the past to reach the lowest income people, to counteract their desire for high fertility as a means of alleviating certain adverse conditions.

IV.   Employment and Social Problems

Employment, aside from its role in production of goods and services, is an important source of income and of status or recognition to workers and their families. The inability of large segments of the economically active population in developing countries to find jobs offering a minimum acceptable standard of living is reflected in a widening of income disparities and a deepening sense of economic, political and social frustration.

The most economically significant employment problems in LDCs contributed
to by excessive population growth are low worker productivity in production of traditional goods
and services produced, the changing aspirations of the work force, the existing distribution of
income, wealth and power, and the natural resource endowment of a country.

The political and social problems of urban overcrowding are directly related to population
growth. In addition to the still-high fertility in urban areas of many LDC's, population pressures
on the land, which increases migration to the cities, adds to the pressures on urban job markets
and political stability, and strains, the capacity l to provide schools, health facilities, and water
supplies.

It should be recognized that lower fertility will relieve only a portion of these strains and
that its most beneficial effects will be felt only over a period of decades. Most of the potential
migrants from countryside to city over the coming 15 to 20 years have already been born. Lower
birth rates do provide some immediate relief to health and sanitation and welfare services, and
medium- term relief to pressures on educational systems. The largest effects on employment,
migration, and living standards, however, will be felt only after 25 or 30 years. The time lags
inherent in all
aspects of population dynamics only reinforce the urgency of adopting effective policies in the
years immediately ahead if the formidable problems of the present decade are not to become
utterly unmanageable in the 1990s and beyond the year 2000.

CHAPTER V - <u>Implications of Population Pressures for National Security</u>

It seems well understood that the impact of population factors on the subjects already considered -- development, food requirements, resources, environment -- adversely affects the welfare and progress of countries in which we have a friendly interest and thus indirectly adversely affects broad U.S. interests as well.

The effects of population factors on the political stability of these countries and their implications for internal and international order or disorder, destructive social unrest, violence and disruptive foreign activities are less well understood and need more analysis. Nevertheless, some strategists and experts believe that these effects may ultimately be the most important of those arising from population factors, most harmful to the countries where they occur and seriously affecting U.S. interests. Other experts within the U.S. Government disagree with this conclusion.

A recent study* of forty-five local conflicts involving Third World countries examined the ways in which population factors affect the initiation and course of a conflict in different situations. The study reached two major conclusions:

1. ". . . population factors are indeed critical in, and often determinants of, violent conflict in developing areas. Segmental (religious, social, racial) differences, migration, rapid population growth, differential levels of knowledge and skills, rural/urban differences, population pressure and the special location of population in relation to resources -- in this rough order of importance -- all appear to be important contributions to conflict and violence...

2. Clearly, conflicts which are regarded in primarily political terms often have demographic roots: Recognition of these relationships appears crucial to any understanding or prevention of such hostilities."

It does not appear that the population factors act alone or, often, directly to cause the disruptive effects. They act through intervening elements -- variables. They also add to other causative factors turning what might have been only a difficult situation into one with disruptive results.

---

* Choucri, Nazli, Professor of Political Science, M.I.T. - "Population Dynamics and Local Conflict; A Cross-National Study of Population and War, A Summary," June 1974.

This action is seldom simple. Professor Philip Hauser of the University of Chicago has suggested the concept of "population complosion" to describe the situation in many developing countries when (a) more and more people are born into or move into and are compressed in the same living space under (b) conditions and irritations of different races, colours, religions, languages, or cultural backgrounds, often with differential rates of population growth among these groups, and (c) with the frustrations of failure to achieve their aspirations for better standards of living for themselves or their children. To these may be added pressures for and actual international migration. These population factors appear to have a multiplying effect on other factors involved in situations of incipient violence. Population density, the "overpopulation" most often thought of in this connection, is much less important.

These population factors contribute to socio-economic variables including breakdowns in social structures, underemployment and unemployment, poverty, deprived people in city slums, lowered I opportunities for education for the masses, few job opportunities for those who do obtain education, interracial, religious, and regional rivalries, and sharply increased financial, planning, and administrative burdens on governmental systems at all levels.

These adverse conditions appear to contribute frequently to harmful developments of a political nature: Juvenile delinquency, thievery and other crimes, organized brigandry, kidnapping and terrorism, food riots, other outbreaks of violence; guerrilla warfare, communal violence, separatist movements, revolutionary movements and counter-revolutionary coupe. All of these bear upon the weakening or collapse of local, state, or national government functions.

Beyond national boundaries, population factors appear to have had operative roles in some past politically disturbing legal or illegal mass migrations, border incidents, and wars. If current increased population pressures continue they may have greater potential for future disruption in foreign relations.

Perhaps most important, in the last decade population factors have impacted more severely than before on availabilities of agricultural land and resources, industrialization, pollution and the environment. All this is occurring at a time when international communications have created rising expectations which are being frustrated by slow development and inequalities of distribution.

Since population factors work with other factors and act through intervening linkages, research as to their effects of a political nature is difficult and "proof" even more so. This does not mean, however, that the causality does not exist. It means only that U.S. policy decisions must take into account the less precise and programmatic character of our knowledge of these linkages.

Although general hypotheses are hard to draw, some seem reasonably sustainable:

1.   Population growth and inadequate resources. Where population size is greater than available resources, or is expanding more rapidly than the available resources, there is a

tendency toward internal disorders and violence and, sometimes, disruptive international policies or violence. The higher the rate of growth, the more salient a factor population increase appears to be. A sense of increasing crowding, real or perceived, seems to generate such tendencies, especially if it seems to thwart obtaining desired personal or national goals.

2.   Populations with a high proportion of growth. The young people, who are in much higher proportions in many LDCs, are likely to be more volatile, unstable, prone to extremes, alienation and violence than an older population. These young people can more readily be persuaded to attack the legal institutions of the government or real property of the "establishment," "imperialists," multinational corporations, or other — often foreign — influences blamed for their troubles.

3.   Population factors with social cleavages. When adverse population factors of growth, movement, density, excess, or pressure coincide with racial, religious, color, linguistic, cultural, or other social cleavages, there will develop the most potentially explosive situations for internal disorder, perhaps with external effects. When such factors exist together with the reality or sense of relative deprivation among different groups within the same country or in relation to other countries or peoples, the probability of violence increases significantly.

4.   Population movements and international migrations. Population movements within countries appear to have a large role in disorders. Migrations into neighbouring countries (especially those richer or more sparsely settled), whether legal or illegal, can provoke negative political reactions or force.

There may be increased propensities for violence arising simply from technological developments making it easier — e.g., international proliferation and more ready accessibility to sub-national groups of nuclear and other lethal weaponry. These possibilities make the disruptive population factors discussed above even more dangerous.

Some Effects of Current Population Pressures

In the 1960s and 1970s, there have been a series of episodes in which population factors have apparently had a role — directly or indirectly — affecting countries in which we have an interest.

El Salvador-Honduras War. An example was the 1969 war between El Salvador and Honduras. Dubbed the "Soccer War", it was sparked by a riot during a soccer match, its underlying cause was tension resulting from the large scale migration of Salvadorans from their rapidly growing, densely populated country to relatively uninhabited areas of Honduras. The Hondurans resented the presence of migrants and in 1969 began to enforce an already extant land tenancy law to expel them. El Salvador was angered by the treatment given its citizens. Flaring tempers on both sides over this issue created a situation which ultimately led to a military clash.

Nigeria. The Nigerian civil war seriously retarded the progress of Africa's most populous nations and caused political repercussions and pressures in the United States. It was fundamentally a matter of tribal relationships. Irritations among the tribes caused in part by rapidly increasing numbers of people, in a situation of inadequate opportunity for most of them, magnified the tribal issues and may have helped precipitate the war. The migration of the Ibos from Eastern Nigeria, looking for employment, led to competition with local peoples of other tribes and contributed to tribal rioting. This unstable situation was intensified by the fact that in the 1963 population census returns were falsified to inflate the Western region's population and hence its representation in the Federal Government. The Ibos of the Eastern region, with the oil resources of the country, felt their resources would be unjustly drawn on and attempted to establish their independence.

Pakistan-India-Bangladesh 1970-71. This religious and nationalistic conflict contains several points where a population factor at a crucial time may have had a causal effect in turning events away from peaceful solutions to violence. The Central Government in West Pakistan resorted to military suppression of the East Wing after the election in which the Awami League had an overwhelming victory in East Pakistan. This election had followed two sets of circumstances. The first was a growing discontent in East Pakistan at the slow rate of economic and social progress being made and the Bengali feeling that West Pakistan was dealing unequally and unfairly with East Pakistan in the distribution of national revenues. The first population factor was the 75 million Bengalis whom the 45 million West Pakistanis sought to continue to dominate. Some observers believe that as a recent population factor the rapid rate of population growth in East Pakistan seriously diminished the per capita improvement from the revenues made available and contributed significantly to the discontent. A special aspect of the population explosion in East Pakistan (second population factor) was the fact that the dense occupation of all good agricultural land forced hundreds of thousands of people to move into the obviously unsafe lowlands along the southern coast. They became victims of the hurricane in 1970. An estimated 300,000 died. The Government was unable to deal with a disaster affecting so many people. The leaders and people of East Pakistan reacted vigorously to this failure of the Government to bring help.

It seems quite likely that these situations in which population factors played an important role led to the overwhelming victory of the Awami League that led the Government to resort to force in East Pakistan with the massacres and rapes that followed. Other experts believe the effects of the latter two factors were of marginal influence in the Awami League's victory.

It further seems possible that much of the violence was stimulated or magnified by population pressures. Two groups of Moslems had been competing for jobs and land in East Bengal since the 1947 partition. "Biharis" are a small minority of non-Bengali Moslems who chose to resettle in East Pakistan at that time. Their integration into Bengali society was undoubtedly inhibited by the deteriorating living conditions of the majority Bengalis. With the Pakistan army crackdown in March, 1971, the Biharis cooperated with the authorities, and reportedly were able thereby to improve their economic conditions at the expense of the persecuted Bengalis. When the tables were turned after independence, it was the Biharis who were persecuted and whose property and jobs were seized. It seems likely that both these outbursts of violence were induced or enlarged by the population "complosion" factor. The violence in East Pakistan against the Bengalis and particularly the Hindu minority who bore the brunt of Army repression led to the next population factor, the mass migration during one year of nine or ten million refugees into West Bengal in India. This placed a tremendous burden on the already weak Indian economy. As one Indian leader in the India Family Planning Program said, "The influx of nine million people wiped out the savings of some nine million births which had been averted over a period of eight years of the family planning program."

There were other factors in India's invasion of East Bengal, but it is possible that the necessity of returning these nine or ten million ~ refugees to east Bengal -- getting them out of India — may have I played a part in the Indian decision to invade. Certainly, in a I broader sense, the threat posed by this serious, spreading instability I on India's eastern frontier -- an instability in which population factors were a major underlying cause -- a key reason for the Indian decision.

The political arrangements in the Subcontinent have changed, but all of the underlying population factors which influenced the dramatic acts of violence that took place in 1970-71 still exist, in worsening dimensions, to influence future events.

Additional illustrations. Population factors also appear to have had indirect causal relations, in varying degrees, on the killings in Indonesia in 1965-6, the communal slaughter in Rwanda in 1961-2 and 1963-4 and in Burundi in 1972, the coup in Uganda in 1972, and the insurrection in Sri Lanka in 1971.

Some Potential Effects of Future Population Pressures

Between the end of World War II and 1975 the world's population will have increased about one and a half billion -- nearly one billion of that from 1960 to the present. The rate of growth is increasing and between two and a half and three and a half billion will be added by the year 2000, depending partly on the effectiveness of population growth control programs. This increase of the next 25 years will, of course, pyramid on the great number added with such rapidity in the last 25. The population factors which contributed to the political pressures and instabilities of the last decades will be multiplied.

PRC - The demographic factors of the PRC are referred to on page 79 above. The Government of the PRC has made a major effort to feed its growing population.

Cultivated farm land, at 107 million hectares, has not increased significantly over the past 25 years, although farm output has substantially kept pace with population growth through improved yields secured by land improvement, irrigation extension, intensified cropping, and rapid expansion in the supply of fertilizers.

In 1973 the PRC adopted new, forceful population control measures. In the urban areas

Peking claimed its birth control measures had secured a two-child family and a one percent annual population growth, and it proposes to extend this development throughout the rural areas by 1980.

The political implications of China's future population growth are obviously important but are not dealt with here.

Israel and the Arab States.   If a peace settlement can be reached, the central issue will be how to make it last. Egypt with about 37 million today is growing at 2.8% per year. It will approximate 48 million by 1985, 75 million by 1995, and more than 85 million by 2000. It is doubtful that Egypt's economic progress can greatly exceed its population growth. With Israel starting at today's population of 3.3 million, the disparity between its population and those of the Arab States will rapidly increase. Inside Israel, unless Jewish immigration continues, the gap between the size of the Arab and Jewish populations will diminish. Together with the traditional animosities — which will remain the prime determinants of Arab-Israeli conflict — these population factors make the potential for peace and for U.S. interests in the area ominous.

India-Bangladesh.   The Subcontinent will be for years the major focus of world concern over population growth. India's population is now approximately 580 million, adding a million by each full moon. Embassy New Delhi (New Delhi 2115, June 17,1974) reports:

> "There seems no way of turning off the faucet this side of 1 billion Indians, which means India must continue to court economic and social disaster. It is not clear how the shaky and slow-growing Indian economy can bear the enormous expenditures on health, housing, employment, and education, which must be made if the society is even to maintain its current low levels."

Death rates have recently increased in parts of India and episodes like the recent smallpox epidemic have led Embassy New Delhi to add:

> "A future failure of the India food crop could cause widespread death and suffering which could not be overcome by the GOI or foreign assistance. The rise in the death rate in several rural areas suggests that Malthusian pressures are already being felt."

And further:

> "Increasing political disturbances should be expected in the future, fed by the pressures of rising population in urban areas, food shortages, and growing scarcities in household commodities. The GOI has not been very successful in alleviating unemployment in the cities. The recent disturbances in Gujarat and Bihar seem to be only the beginning of chronic and serious political disorders occurring throughout India."

There will probably be a weakening, possibly a breakdown, of the control of the central government over some of the states and local areas. The democratic system will be taxed and may be in danger of giving way to a form of dictatorship, benevolent or otherwise. The existence of India as a democratic buttress in Asia will be threatened.

Bangladesh.   With appalling population density, rapid population growth, and extensive poverty will suffer even more. Its population has increased 40% since the census 13 years ago and is growing at least 3% per year. The present 75 million, or so, unless slowed by famine, disease, or massive birth control, will double in 23 years and exceed 170 million by 2000.

Requirements for food and other basic necessities of life are growing at a faster rate than existing resources and administrative systems are providing them. In the rural areas, the size of the average farm is being reduced and there is increasing landlessness. More and more people are migrating to urban areas. The government admits a 30% rate of unemployment and underemployment. Already, Embassy Dacca reports (Dacca 3424, June 19, 1974) there are important economic-population causes for the landlessness that is rapidly increasing and contributing to violent crimes of murder and armed robbery that terrorize the ordinary citizen.

"Some of the vast army of unemployed and landless, and those strapped by
the escalating cost of basic commodities, have doubtless turned to crime."

Three paragraphs of Embassy Dacca's report sharply outline the effect on U.S. political interests we may anticipate from population I factors in Bangladesh and other countries that, if present trends are not changed, will be in conditions similar to Bangladesh in only a few years.

"Of concern to the U.S. are several probable outcomes as the basic political, economic and social situation worsens over the coming decades. Already afflicted with a crisis mentality by which they look to wealthy foreign countries to shore up their faltering economy, the BDG will continue to escalate its demands on the U.S. both bilaterally and internationally to enlarge its assistance, both of commodities and financing. Bangladesh is now a fairly solid supporter of third world positions, advocating better distribution of the world's wealth and extensive trade concessions to poor nations. As its problems grow and its ability to gain assistance fails to keep pace, Bangladesh's positions on international issues likely will become radicalized, inevitably in opposition to U.S. interests on major issues as it seeks to align itself with others to force adequate aid.

"U.S. interests in Bangladesh center on the development of an economically and politically stable country which will not threaten the stability of its neighbours in the Subcontinent nor invite the intrusion of outside powers. Surrounded on three sides by India and sharing a short border with Burma, Bangladesh, if it descends into chaos, will threaten the stability of these nations as well. Already Bengalees are illegally migrating into the frontier provinces of Assam and Tripura, politically sensitive areas of India, and into adjacent Burma. Should expanded out-migration and socio-political collapse in Bangladesh threaten its own stability, India may be forced to consider intervention, although it is difficult to see in what way the Indians could cope with the situation.

"Bangladesh is a case study of the effects of few resources and burgeoningpopulation not only on national and regional stability but also on the future world order. In a sense, if we and other richer elements of the world community do not meet the test of formulating a policy to help Bangladesh awaken from its economic and demographic nightmare, we will not be prepared in future decades to deal with the consequences of similar problems in other countries which have far more political and economic consequences to U.S. interests."

Africa--Sahel Countries. The current tragedy of the Sahel countries, to which U.S. aid in past years has been minimal, has suddenly cost us an immense effort in food supplies at a time when we are already hard pressed to supply other countries, and domestic food prices are causing strong political repercussions in the U.S. The costs to us and other donor countries for aid to help restore the devastated land will run into hundreds of millions. Yet little attention is given to the fact that even before the adverse effect of the continued drought, it was population growth and added migration of herdsmen to the edge of the desert that led to cutting the trees and cropping the grass, inviting the desert to sweep forward. Control of population growth and migration must be a part of any program for improvement of lasting value.

Panama. The troublesome problem of jurisdiction over the Canal Zone is primarily due to Panamanian feelings of national pride and a desire to achieve sovereignty over its entire territory. One Panamanian agreement in pursuing its treaty goals is that U.S control over the Canal Zone prevents the natural expansion of Panama City, an expansion needed as a result of demographic pressures. In 1908, at the time of the construction of the Canal, the population of the Zone was about 40,000. Today it is close to the same figure, 45,000. On the other hand, Panama City, which had some 20,000 people in 1908, has received growing migration from rural areas and now has over 500,000. A new treaty which would give Panama jurisdiction over land now in the Zone would help alleviate the problems caused by this growth of Panama City.

Mexico and the U.S. Closest to home, the combined population growth of Mexico and the U.S. Southwest presages major difficulties for the future. Mexico's population is growing at some 3.5% per year and will double in 20 years with concomitant increases in demands for food, housing, education, and employment. By 1995, the present 57 million will have increased to some 115 million and, unless their recently established family planning program has great success, by 2000 will exceed 130 million. More important, the numbers of young people entering the job market each year will expand even more quickly. These growing numbers will increase the pressure of illegal emigration to the U.S., and make the issue an even more serious source of friction in our political relations with Mexico.

On our side, the Bureau of the Census estimates that as more and more Americans move to the Southwestern States the present 40,000,000 population may approximate 61,000,000 by 1995. The domestic use of Colorado River water may again have increased the salinity level in Mexico and reopened that political issue.

Amembassy Mexico City (Mexico 4953, June 14, 1974) summarized the influences of population factors on U.S. interests as follows:

"An indefinite continuation of Mexico's high population growth rate would increasingly act as a brake on economic (and social) improvement. The consequences would be noted in various ways. Mexico could well take more radical positions in the international scene. Illegal migration to the U.S. would increase. In a country where unemployment and under-employment is already high, the entry of increasing numbers into the work force would only intensify the pressure to seek employment in the U.S. by whatever means. Yet another consequence would be increased demand for food imports from the U.S., especially if the fate of growth of agricultural production continues to lag behind the population growth rate. Finally, one cannot dismiss the spectre of future domestic instability as a long term consequence, should the economy, now strong, falter."

UNCTAD, the Special UNGA, and the UN. The developing countries, after several years of unorganized maneuvering and erratic attacks have now formed tight groupings in the Special Committee for Latin American Coordination, the Organization of African States, and the Seventy-Seven. As illustrated in the Declaration of Santiago and the recent Special General Assembly, these groupings at times appear to reflect a common desire to launch economic attacks against the United States and, to a lesser degree, the European developed countries. A factor which is common to all of them, which retards their development, burdens their foreign exchange, subjects them to world prices for food, fertilizer, and necessities of life and pushes them into disadvantageous trade relations is their excessively rapid population growth. Until they are able to overcome this problem, it is likely that their manifestations of antagonism toward the United States in international bodies will increase.

Global Factors

In industrial nations, population growth increases demand for industrial output. This over time tends to deplete national raw materials resources and calls increasingly on sources of marginal profitability and foreign supplies. To obtain raw materials, industrial nations seek to locate and develop external sources of supply. The potential for collisions of interest among the developing countries is obvious and has already begun. It is visible and vexing in claims for territorial waters and national sovereignty over mineral resources. It may become intense in rivalries over exploring and exploiting the resources of the ocean floor.

In developing countries, the burden of population factors, added to others, will weaken unstable governments, often only marginally effective in good times, and open the way for extremist regimes.

Countries suffering under such burdens will be more susceptible to radicalization. Their vulnerability also might invite foreign intervention by stronger nations bent on acquiring political and economic advantage. The tensions within the Have-not nations are likely to intensify, and the conflicts between them and the Haves may escalate.

Past experience gives little assistance to predicting the course of these developments because the speed of today's population growth, migrations, and urbanization far exceeds anything the world has seen before. Moreover, the consequences of such population factors can no longer be evaded by moving to new hunting or grazing lands, by conquering new territory, by discovering or colonizing new continents, or by emigration in large numbers.

The world has ample warning that we all must make more rapid efforts at social and economic development to avoid or mitigate these gloomy prospects. We should be warned also that we all must move as rapidly as possible toward stabilizing national and world population growth.

CHAPTER VI - <u>World Population Conference</u>

From the standpoint of policy and program, the focal point of the World Population Conference (WPC) at Bucharest, Romania, in August 1974, was the World Population Plan of Action (WPPA) The U.S. had contributed many substantive points to the draft Plan We had particularly emphasized the incorporation of population factors in national planning of developing countries' population programs for assuring the availability of means of family planning to persons of reproductive age, voluntary but specific goals for the reduction of population growth and time frames for action

As the WPPA reached the WPC it was organized as a demographic document. It also related population factors to family welfare, social and economic development, and fertility reduction. Population policies and programs were recognized as an essential element, but only one element of economic and social development programs. The sovereignty of nations in determining their own population policies and programs was repeatedly recognized. The general impression after five regional consultative meetings on the Plan was that it had general support.

There was general consternation, therefore, when at the beginning of the conference the Plan was subjected to a slashing, five-pronged attack led by Algeria, with the backing of several African countries; Argentina, supported by Uruguay, Brazil, Peru and, more limitedly, some other Latin American countries; the Eastern European group (less Romania); the PRC and the Holy See. Although the attacks were not identical, they embraced three central elements relevant to U.S. policy and action in this field:

1. Repeated references to the importance (or as some said, the pre- condition) of economic and social development for the reduction of high fertility. Led by Algeria and Argentina, many emphasized the "new international economic order" as central to economic and social development.

2. Efforts to reduce the references to population programs, minimize their importance and delete all references to quantitative or time goals.

3. Additional references to national sovereignty in setting population policies and programs.

The Plan of Action

Despite the initial attack and continuing efforts to change the conceptual basis of the world Population Plan of Action, the Conference adopted by acclamation (only the Holy See staking a general reservation) a complete World Population Plan of Action. It is less urgent in tone than the draft submitted by the U.N. Secretariat but in several ways more complete and with greater potential than that draft. The final action followed a vigorous debate with hotly contested positrons and forty-seven votes. Nevertheless, there was general satisfaction among the participants at the success of their efforts.

a. Principles and Aims

The Plan of Action lays down several important principles, some for the first time in a U.N. document.

1. Among the first-time statements is the assertion that the sovereign right of each nation to set its own population policies is "to be exercised ... taking into account universal solidarity in order to improve the quality of life of the peoples of the world." (Pare 13) This new provision opens the way toward increasing responsibility by nations toward other nations in establishing their national population policies.

2. The conceptual relationship between population and development is stated in Para 13(c):

> Population and development are interrelated: population variables influence development variables and are also influenced by them; the formulation of a World Population Plan of Action reflects the international community's awareness of the importance of population trends for socio-economic development, and the socio-economic nature of the recommendations contained in this Plan of Action reflects its awareness of the crucial role that development plays in affecting population trends.

3. A basic right of couples and individuals is recognized by Para 13(f), for the first time in a single declarative sentence:

> All couples and individuals have the basic human right to decide freely and responsibly the number and spacing of their children and to have the information, education and means to do so;

4. Also for the first time, a U.N. document links the responsibility of child-bearers to the community [Para 13(f) continued]:

> The responsibility of couples and individuals in the exercise of this right takes into account the needs of their living and future children, and their responsibilities towards the community.

It is now possible to build on this newly-stated principle as the right of couples first recognized in the Tehran Human Rights Declaration of 1968 has been built on.

5. A flat declaration of the right of women is included in Para 13(h):

> Women have the right to complete integration in the development process particularly by means of an equal participation in educational, social, economic, cultural and political life. In addition, the necessary measures should be taken to facilitate this

integration with family responsibilities which should be fully shared by both partners.

6. The need for international action is accepted in Para 13(k):

The growing interdependence of countries makes the adoption of measures at the international level increasingly important for the solution of problems of development and population problems.

7. The "primary aim" of the Plan of Action is asserted to be "to expand and deepen the capacities of countries to deal effectively with their national and subnational population problems and to promote an appropriate international response to their needs by increasing international activity in research, the exchange of information, and the provision of assistance on request."

b. Recommendations

The Plan of Action includes recommendations for: population goals and policies; population growth; mortality and morbidity; reproduction; family formation and the status of women; population distribution and internal migration; international migration; population structure; socio-economic policies; data collection and analysis; research; development and evolution of population policies; the role of national governments and of international cooperation; and monitoring, review and appraisal.

A score of these recommendations are the most important:

1. Governments should integrate population measures and programs into omprehensive social and economic plans and programs and their integration should be reflected in the goals, instrumentalities and organizations for planning within the countries. A unit dealing with population aspects should be created and placed at a high level of the national administrative structure. (Para 94)

2. Countries which consider their population growth hampers attainment of their goals should consider adopting population policies -- through a low level of birth and death rates. (Para 17,18)

3. Highest priority should be given to reduction in mortality and morbidity and increase of life expectancy and programs for this purpose should reach rural areas and underprivileged groups. (Para 20-25)

4.   Countries are urged to encourage appropriate education concerning responsible parenthood and make available to persons who so desire advice and means of achieving it. [Pare 29(b)]

5.   Family planning and related services should aim at prevention of unwanted pregnancies and also at elimination of involuntary sterility or subfecundity to enable couples to achieve their desired number of children.   [Pare 29 (c)]

6.   Adequately trained auxiliary personnel, social workers and non-government channels should be used to help provide family planning services. [Pare 29(e)]

7.   Governments with family planning programs should consider coordinating them with health and other services designed to raise the quality of life.

8.   Countries wishing to affect fertility levels should give priority to development programs and health and education strategies which have a decisive effect upon demographic trends, including fertility. [Pare 31] International cooperation should give priority to assisting such national efforts. Such programs may include reduction in infant and child mortality, increased education, particularly for females, improvement in the status of women, land reform and support in old age. [Para 32]

9.   Countries which consider their birth rates detrimental to their national purposes are invited to set quantitative goals and implement policies to achieve them by 1985. [Pare 37]

10.   Developed countries are urged to develop appropriate policies in population, consumption and investment, bearing in mind the need for fundamental improvement in international equity.

11.   Because the family is the basic unit of society, governments should assist families as far as possible through legislation and services. [Para 39]

12.   Governments should ensure full participation of women in the educational, economic, social and political life of their countries on an equal basis with men. [Pare 40] (A new provision, added at Bucharest.)

13.   A series of recommendations are made to stabilize migration within countries, particularly policies to reduce the undesirable consequences of excessively rapid urbanization and to develop opportunities in rural areas and small towns, recognizing the right of individuals to move freely within their national boundaries. [Para 44-50]

14.   Agreements should be concluded to regulate the international migration of workers and to assure non-discriminatory treatment and social services for these workers and

their families; also other measures to decrease the brain drain from developing countries. [Para 51-62]

15.   To assure needed information concerning population trends, population censuses should be taken at regular intervals and information concerning births and deaths be made available at feast annually. [Para 72-77]

16.   Research should be intensified to develop knowledge concerning the social, economic and political interrelationships with population trends; effective means of reducing infant and childhood mortality; methods for integrating population goals into national plans, means of improving the motivation of people, analysis of population policies in relation to socio-economic development, laws and institution; methods of fertility regulation to meet the varied requirement of individuals and communities, including methods requiring no medical supervision; the interrelations of health, nutrition and reproductive biology; and utilization of social services, including family planning services. [Para 78-80]

17.   Training of management on population dynamics and administration, on an interdisciplinary basis, should be provided for medical, paramedical, traditional health personnel, program administrators, senior government officials, labor, community and social leaders. Education and information programs should be undertaken to bring population information to all areas of countries. [Paras 81-92]

18.   An important role of governments is to determine and assess the population problems and needs of their countries in the light of their political, social, cultural, religious and economic conditions; such an undertaking should be carried out systematically and periodically so as to provide informed, rational and dynamic decision-making in matters of population and development. [Para 97]

20.   The Plan of Action should be closely coordinated with the International Development Strategy for the Second United Nations Development Decade, reviewed in depth at five year intervals, and modified as appropriate. [Pares 106-108]

The Plan of Action hedges in presenting specific statements of quantitative goals or a time frame for the reduction of fertility. These concepts are included, however, in the combination of Paras 16 and 36, together with goals [Pare 37] and the review [Pare 106]. Para 16 states that, according to the U.N low variant projections, it is estimated that as a result of social and economic development and population policies as reported by countries in the Second United Nations Inquiry on Population and Development, population growth rates in the developing countries as a whole may decline from the present level of 2.4% per annum to about 2% by 1985; and below 0.7% per annum in the developed countries. In this case the worldwide rate of population growth would decline from 2% to about 1.7%. Para 36 says that these projections and those for mortality decline are consistent with declines in the birth rate of the developing countries as a whole from the present level of 38 per thousand to 30 per thousand by 1985. Para 36 goes on to say that "To achieve by 1985 these levels of fertility would require substantial national efforts, by those countries concerned, in the field of socio-economic development and population policies, supported, upon request, by adequate international assistance." Para 37 then follows with the statement that countries which consider their birth rates detrimental to their national purposes are invited to consider setting quantitative goals and implementing policies that may lead to the attainment of such goals by 1985. Para 106 recommends a comprehensive review and appraisal of population trends and policies discussed in the Plan of Action should be undertaken every five years and modified, wherever needed, by ECOSOC.

Usefulness of the Plan of Action

The World Population Plan of Action, despite its wordiness and often hesitant tone, contains all the necessary provisions for effective population growth control programs at national and international levels. It lacks only plain statements of quantitative goals with time frames for their accomplishment. These will have to be added by individual national action and development as rapidly as possible in further U.N. documents. The basis for suitable goals exists in paragraphs 16, 36, 37, and 106,
referred to above. The U.N. low variant projection used in these paragraphs is close to the goals proposed by the United States and other ECAFE nations:

- For developed countries -
    replacement levels of fertility by 1985; stationary populations as soon as practicable.

- For developing countries -
    replacement levels in two or three decades.

- For the world -
    a 1.7% population growth rate by 1985 with 2% average for the developing countries and 0.7% average for developed countries; replacement level of fertility for all countries by 2000.

The dangerous situation evidenced by the current food situation and projections for the future make it essential to press for the realization of these goals. The beliefs, ideologies and misconceptions displayed by many nations at Bucharest indicate more forcefully than ever the need for extensive education of the leaders of many governments, especially in Africa and some in Latin America. Approaches leaders of individual countries must tee designed in the light of their current beliefs and to meet their special concerns. These might include:

1. Projections of population growth individualized for countries and with analyses of relations of population factors to social and economic development of each country.

2. Familiarization programs at U.N. Headquarters in New York for ministers of governments, senior policy level officials and comparably influential leaders from private life.

3. Greatly increased training programs for senior officials in the elements of

demographic economics.

    4. Assistance in integrating population factors in national plans, particularly as they relate to health services, education, agricultural resources and development, employment, equitable distribution of income and social stability.

    5. Assistance in relating population policies and family planning programs to major sectors of development: health, nutrition, agriculture, education, social services, organized labor, women's activities, community development.

    6. Initiatives to implement the Percy amendment regarding improvement in the status of women.

    7. Emphasis in assistance and development programs on development of ruralareas.

    All these activities and others particularly productive are consistent with the Plan of Action and may be based upon it.

    Beyond these activities, essentially directed at national interests, a broader educational concept is needed to convey an acute understanding of the interrelation of national interests and world population growth.

PART TWO

Policy Recommendations

I. Introduction - A U.S. Global Population Strategy

There is no simple single approach to the population problem which will provide a "technological fix". As the previous analysis makes clear the problem of population growth has social, economic and technological aspects all of which must be understood and dealt with for a world population policy to succeed. With this in mind, the following broad recommended strategy provides a framework for the development of specific individual programs which must be tailored to the needs and particularities of each country and of different sectors of the population within a country. Essentially all its recommendations made below are supported by the World Population Plan of action drafted at the World Population Conference.

A. Basic Global Strategy

The following basic elements are necessary parts of a comprehensive approach to the population problem which must include both bilateral and multilateral components to achieve success. Thus, USG population assistance programs will need to be coordinated with those of the major multilateral institutions, voluntary organizations, and other bilateral donors.

The common strategy for dealing with rapid population growth should encourage constructive actions to lower fertility since population growth over the years will seriously negate reasonable prospects for the sound social and economic development of the peoples involved.

While the time horizon in this NSSM is the year 2000 we must recognize that in most countries, especially the LDCs, population stability cannot be achieved until the next century. There are too many powerful socio-economic factors operating on family size decisions and too much momentum built into the dynamics of population growth to permit a quick and dramatic reversal of current trends. There is also even less cause for optimism on the rapidity of socio-economic progress that would generate rapid fertility reduction in the poor LDCs than on the feasibility of extending family planning services to those in their populations who may wish to take advantage of them. Thus, at this point we cannot know with certainty when world population can feasibly be stabilized, nor can we state with assurance the limits of the world's ecological "carrying capability". But we can be certain of the desirable direction of change and can state as a plausible objective the target of achieving replacement fertility rates by the year 2000.

Over the past few years, U.S. government-funded population programs have played a major role in arousing interest in family planning in many countries, and in launching and accelerating the growth of national family planning programs. In most countries, there has been an initial rapid growth in contraceptive "acceptors" up to perhaps 10% of fertile couples in a few LDCs. The acceleration of previous trends of fertility decline is attributable, at least in part, to family planning programs.

However, there is growing appreciation that the problem is more long term and complex than first appeared and that a short term burst of activity or moral fervour will not solve it. The danger in this realization is that the U.S. might abandon its commitment to assisting in the world's population problem, rather than facing up to it for the long-run difficult problem that it is.

From year to year we are learning more about what kind of fertility reduction is feasible in differing LDC situations. Given the laws of compound growth, even comparatively small reductions in fertility over the next decade will make a significant difference in total numbers by the year 2000, and a far more significant one by the year 2050.

The proposed strategy calls for a coordinated approach to respond to the important U.S. foreign policy interest in the influence of population growth on the world's political, economic and ecological systems. What is unusual about population is that this foreign policy interest must have a time horizon far beyond that of most other objectives. While there are strong short-run reasons for population programs, because of such factors as food supply, pressures on social service budgets, urban migration and social and political instability, the major impact of the benefits - or avoidance of catastrophe - that could be accomplished by a strengthened U.S. commitment in the population area will be felt less by those of us in the U.S. and other countries today than by our children and grandchildren.

B.   Key Country priorities in U.S. and Multilateral Population Assistance

One issue in any global population strategy is the degree of emphasis in allocation of program resources among countries. The options available range from heavy concentration on a few vital large countries to a geographically diverse program essentially involving all countries willing to accept such assistance. All agencies believe the following policy provides the proper overall balance.

In order to assist the development of major countries and to maximize progress toward population stability, primary emphasis would be placed on the largest and fastest growing developing countries where the imbalance between growing numbers and development potential most seriously risks instability, unrest, and international tensions. These countries are: India, Bangladesh, Pakistan, Nigeria, Mexico, Indonesia, Brazil, The Philippines, Thailand, Egypt, Turkey, Ethiopia, and Colombia.   Out of a total 73.3 million worldwide average increase in population from 1970-75 these countries contributed 34.3 million or 47%. This group of priority countries includes some with virtually no government interest in family planning and others with active government family planning programs which require and would welcome enlarged technical and financial assistance. These countries should be given the highest priority within AID's population program in terms of resource allocations and/or leadership efforts to encourage action by other donors and organizations.

However, other countries would not be ignored. AID would provide population assistance and/ or undertake leadership efforts with respect to other, lower priority countries to the extent that the availability of funds and staff permits, taking into account of such factors as: long run U.S. political interests; impact of rapid population growth on its development potential; the country's relative contribution to world population growth; its financial capacity to cope with the problem; potential impact on domestic unrest and international frictions (which can apply to small as well as large countries); its significance as a test or demonstration case; and opportunities for expenditures that appear particularly cost-effective (e.g. it has been suggested that there may be particularly cost-effective opportunities for supporting family planning to reduce the lag between mortality and fertility declines in countries where death rates are still declining rapidly); national commitment to an effective program.

For both the high priority countries and the lower priority ones to which funds and staff permit aid, the form and content of our assistance or leadership efforts would vary from country to country, depending on each nation's particular interests, needs, and receptivity to various forms of assistance. For example, if these countries are receptive to U.S. assistance through bilateral or central AID funding, we should provide such assistance at levels commensurate with the recipient's capability to finance needed actions with its own funds, the contributions of other donors and organizations, and the effectiveness with which funds can be used.

In countries where U.S. assistance is limited either by the nature of political or diplomatic relations with those countries or by lack of strong government desire. In population reduction programs, external technical and financial assistance (if desired by the countries) would have to come from other donors and/or from private and international organizations, many of which receive contributions from AID. The USG would, however, maintain an interest (e.g. through Embassies) in such countries population problems and programs (if any) to reduce population growth rates. Moreover, particularly in the case of high priority countries, we should be alert to opportunities for expanding our assistance efforts and for demonstrating to their leaders the consequences of rapid population growth and the benefits of actions to reduce fertility.

In countries to which other forms of U.S. assistance are provided but not population assistance, AID will monitor progress toward achievement of development objectives, taking into account the extent to which these are hindered by rapid population growth, and will look for opportunities to encourage initiation of or improvement in population policies and programs.

In addition, the U.S. strategy should support in these LDC countries general activities (e.g. bio-medical research or fertility control methods) capable of achieving major breakthroughs in key problems which hinder reductions in population growth.

C.   Instruments and Modalities for Population Assistance

Bilateral population assistance is the largest and most invisible "instrument" for carrying out U.S. policy in this area. Other instruments include: support for and coordination with population programs of multilateral organizations and voluntary agencies; encouragement of multilateral country consortia and consultative groups to emphasize family planning in reviews of overall recipient progress and aid requests; and formal and informal presentation of views at international gatherings, such as food and population conferences. Specific country strategies must be worked out for each of the highest priority countries, and for the lower priority ones. These strategies will take account of such factors as: national attitudes and sensitivities on family planning; which "instruments" will be most acceptable, opportunities for effective use of assistance; and need of external capital or operating assistance.

For example, in Mexico our strategy would focus on working primarily through private agencies and multilateral organizations to encourage more government attention to the need for control of population growth; in Bangladesh we might provide large-scale technical and financial assistance, depending on the soundness of specific program requests; in Indonesia we would respond to assistance requests but would seek to have Indonesia meet as much of program costs from its own resources (i.e. surplus oil earnings) as possible. In general we would not provide large-scale bilateral assistance in the more developed LDCs, such as Brazil or Mexico. Although these countries are in the top priority list our approach must take account of the fact that their problems relate often to government policies and decisions and not to larger scale need for concessional assistance.

Within the overall array of U.S. foreign assistance programs, preferential treatment in allocation of funds and manpower should be given to cost-effective programs to reduce population growth; including both family planning activities and supportive activities in other sectors.

While some have argued for use of explicit leverage to force better population programs on LDC governments, there are several practical constraints on our efforts to achieve program improvements. Attempts to use "leverage" for far less sensitive issues have generally caused political frictions and often backfired. Successful family planning requires strong local dedication and commitment that cannot over the long run be enforced from the outside. [** *There is also the danger that some LDC leaders will see developed country pressures for family planning as a form of economic or racial imperialism; this could well create a serious backlash.***]

Short of leverage , there are many opportunities, bilaterally and multilaterally, for U.S. representations to discuss and urge the need for stronger family planning programs. There is also some established precedent for taking account of family planning performance in appraisal of assistance requirements by AID and consultative groups. Since population growth is a major determinant of increases in food demand, allocation of scarce PL 480 resources should take account of what steps a country is taking in population control as well as food production. In these sensitive relationships, however, it is important in style as well as substance to avoid the appearance of coercion.

D.   Provision and Development of Family Planning Services,
       Information and Technology

Past experience suggests that easily available family planning services are a vital and effective element in reducing fertility rates in the LDCs.

Two main advances are required for providing safe and effective fertility   control techniques in the developing countries:

1.   Expansion and further development of efficient low-cost systems to assure the full availability of existing family planning services, materials and information to the 85% of LDC populations not now effectively reached. In developing countries willing to create special delivery systems for family planning services this may be the most effective method. In others the most efficient and acceptable method is to combine family planning with health or nutrition in multi-purpose delivery systems.

2.   Improving the effectiveness of present means of fertility control, and developing new technologies which are simple, low cost, effective, safe, long- lasting and acceptable to potential users. This involves both basic developmental research and operations research to judge the utility of new or modified approaches under LDC conditions.

Both of these goals should be given very high priority with necessary additional funding consistent with current or adjusted divisions of labour among other donors and organizations involved in these areas of population assistance.

E. Creating Conditions Conducive to Fertility Decline

It is clear that the availability of contraceptive services and information is not a complete answer to the population problem. In view of the importance of socio-economic factors in determining desired family size, overall assistance strategy should increasingly concentrate on selective policies which will contribute to population decline as well as other goals. This strategy reflects the complementarity between population control and other U.S. development objectives, particularly those relating to AID's Congressional mandate to focus on problems of the poor majority in LDC's.

We know that certain kinds of development policies -- e.g., those which provide the poor with a major share in development benefits -- both promote fertility reductions and accomplish other major development objectives. There are other policies which appear to also promote fertility reduction but which may conflict with non-population objectives (e.g., consider the effect of bringing a large number of women into the labor force in countries and occupations where unemployment is already high and rising).

However, AID knows only approximately the relative priorities among the factors that affect fertility and is even further away from knowing what specific cost-effective steps governments can take to affect these factors.

Nevertheless, with what limited information we have, the urgency of moving forward toward lower fertility rates, even without complete knowledge of the socio-economic forces involved, suggests a three-pronged strategy:

1. High priority to large-scale implementation of programs affecting the determinants of fertility in those cases where there is probable cost- effectiveness, taking account of potential impact on population growth rates; other development benefits to be gained; ethical considerations; feasibility in light of LDC bureaucratic and political concerns and problems; and time-frame for accomplishing objectives.

2. High priority to experimentation and pilot projects in areas where there is evidence of a close relationship to fertility reduction but where there are serious questions about cost-effectiveness relating either to other development impact (e.g., the female employment example cited above) or to program design (e.g., what cost-effective steps can be taken to promote female employment or literacy).

3. High priority to comparative research and evaluation on the relative impact on desired family size of the socio-economic determinants of fertility in general and on what policy scope exists for affecting these determinants.

In all three cases emphasis should be given to moving ction as much as possible to LDC institutions and individuals rather than to involving U.S. researchers on a large scale.

Activities in all three categories would receive very high priority in allocation of AID funds. The largest amounts required should be in the first category and would generally not come from population funds. However, since such activities (e.g., in rural development and basic education) coincide with other AID sectoral priorities, sound project requests from LDC's will be placed close to the top in AID's funding priorities (assuming that they do not conflict with other major development and other foreign policy objectives).

The following areas appear to contain significant promise in effecting fertility declines, and are discussed in subsequent sections.

-- providing minimal levels of education especially for women;

-- reducing infant and child mortality;

-- expanding opportunities for wage employment especially for women;

-- developing alternatives to "social security" support provided by children to aging parents;

-- pursuing development strategies that skew income growth toward
the poor, especially rural development focusing on rural poverty;

-- concentrating on the education and indoctrination of the rising
generation of children regarding the desirability of smaller family size.

The World Population Plan of Action includes a provision (paragraph 31) that countries trying for effective fertility levels should give priority to development programs and health and education strategies which have a decisive effect upon demographic trends, including fertility. It calls for international information to give priority to assisting such national efforts. Programs suggested (paragraph 32) are essentially the same as those listed above.

Food is another of special concern in any population strategy. Adequate food stocks need to be created to provide for periods of severe shortages and LDC food production efforts must be reinforced to meet increased demand resulting from population and income growth. U.S. agricultural production goals should take account of the normal import requirements of LDC's (as well as developed countries) and of likely occasional crop failures in major parts of the LDC world. Without improved food security, there will be pressure leading to possible conflict and the desire for large families for "insurance" purposes, thus undermining other development and population control efforts.

F. Development of World-Wide Political and Popular Commitment
   to Population Stabilization and Its Associated Improvement of
   Individual Quality of Life.

A fundamental element in any overall strategy to deal with the population problem is obtaining the support and commitment of key leaders in the developing countries. This is only possible if they can clearly see the negative impact of unrestricted population growth in their countries and the benefits of reducing birth rates and if they believe it is possible to cope with the population problem through instruments of public policy. Since most high officials are in office for relatively short periods, they have to see early benefits or the value of longer term statesmanship. In each specific case, individual leaders will have to approach their population problems within the context of their country's values, resources, and existing priorities.

Therefore, it is vital that leaders of major LDCs themselves take the lead in advancing family planning and population stabilization, not only within the U.N. and other international organizations but also through bilateral contacts with leaders of other LDCs. Reducing population growth in LDCs should not be advocated exclusively by the developed countries. The U.S. should encourage such a role as opportunities appear in its high level contact with LDC leaders.

The most recent forum for such an effort was the August 1974 U.N. World Population Conference. It was an ideal context to focus concerted world attention on the problem. The debate views and highlights of the World Population Plan of action are reviewed in Chapter VI.

CONFIDENTIAL

The U.S. strengthened its credibility as an advocate of lower population growth rates by explaining that, while it did not have a single written   action population policy, it did have legislation, Executive Branch policies and court decisions that amounted to a national policy and that our national fertility level was already below replacement and seemed likely to attain a stable population by 2000.

The U.S. also proposed to join with other developed countries in an international collaborative effort of research in human reproduction and fertility control covering big-medical and socio-economic factors.

The U.S. further offered to collaborate with other interested donor countries and organizations (e.g., WHO, UNFPA, World Bank, UNICEF) to encourage further action by LDC governments and other institutions to provide low-cost, basic preventive health services, including maternal and child health and family planning services, reaching out into the remote rural areas.

The U.S. delegation also said the U.S. would request from the Congress increased U.S. bilateral assistance to population-family planning programs, and additional amounts for essential functional activities and our contribution to the UNFPA if countries showed an interest in such assistance.

Each of these commitments is important and should be pursued by the U.S. Government.

It is vital that the effort to develop and strengthen a commitment on the part of the LDC leaders not be seen by them as an industrialized country policy to keep their strength down or to reserve resources for use by the "rich" countries. Development of such a perception could create a serious backlash adverse to the cause of population stability. Thus the U.S. and other "rich" countries should take care that policies they advocate for the LDC's would be acceptable within their own countries. (This may require public debate and affirmation of our intended policies.) The "political" leadership role in developing countries should, of course, be taken whenever possible by their own leaders.

The U.S. can help to minimize charges of an imperialist motivation behind its support of population activities by repeatedly asserting that such support derives from a concern with:

> (a)   the right of the individual couple to determine freely and
>   responsibly their number and spacing of children and
>   to have information, education, and means to do so; and

> (b)   the fundamental social and economic development of poor
>   countries in which rapid population growth is both a
>   contributing cause and a consequence of widespread poverty.

Furthermore, the U.S. should also take steps to convey the message that the control of world population growth is in the mutual interest of the developed and developing countries alike.

Family planning programs should be supported by multilateral organizations wherever they can provide the most efficient and acceptable means. Where U.S. bilateral assistance is necessary or preferred, it should be provided in collaboration with host country institutions -- as is the case now. Credit should go to local leaders for the success of projects. The success and acceptability of family planning assistance will depend in large measure on the degree to which it contributes to the ability of the host government to serve and obtain the support of its people.

In many countries today, decision-makers are wary of instituting population programs, not because they are unconcerned about rapid population growth, but because they lack confidence that such programs will succeed. By actively working to demonstrate to such leaders that national population and family planning programs have achieved progress in a wide variety of poor countries, the U.S. could help persuade the leaders of many countries that the investment of funds in national family planning programs is likely to yield high returns even in the short and medium term. Several examples of success exist already, although regrettably they tend to come from LDCs that are untypically well off in terms of income growth and/or social services or are islands or city states.

We should also appeal to potential leaders among the younger generations in developing countries, focusing on the implications of continued rapid population growth for their countries in the next 10-20 years, when they may assume national leadership roles.

Beyond seeking to reach and influence national leaders, improved world-wide support for population-related efforts should be sought through increased emphasis on mass media and other population education and motivation programs by the U.N., USIA, and USAID. We should give higher priorities in our information programs world-wide for this area and consider expansion of collaborative arrangements with multilateral institutions in population education programs.

Another challenge will be in obtaining the further understanding and support of the U.S. public and Congress for the necessary added funds for such an effort, given the competing demands for resources. If an effective program is to be mounted by the U.S., we will need to contribute significant new amounts of funds. Thus there is need to reinforce the positive attitudes of those in Congress who presently support U.S. activity in the population field and to enlist their support in persuading others.
Public debate is needed now.

Personal approaches by the President, the Secretary of State, other members of the Cabinet, and their principal deputies would be helpful in this effort. Congress and the public must be clearly informed that the Executive Branch is seriously worried about the problem and that it deserves their further attention. Congressional representatives at the World Population Conference can help.

CONFIDENTIAL

An Alternative View

The above basic strategy assumes that the current forms of assistance programs in both population and economic and social development areas will be able to solve the problem. There is however, another view, which is shared by a growing number of experts. It believes that the outlook is much harsher and far less tractable than commonly perceived. This holds that the severity of the population problem in this century which is already claiming the lives of more than 10 million people yearly, is such as to make likely continued widespread food shortage and other demographic catastrophes, and, in the words of C.P. Snow, we shall be watching people starve on television.

The conclusion of this view is that mandatory programs may be needed and that we should be considering these possibilities now.

This school of thought believes the following types of questions need to be addressed:

--   Should the U.S. make an all out commitment to major
        limitation of world population with all the financial and
        international as well as domestic political costs that would entail?

--   Should the U.S. set even higher agricultural production goals
        which would enable it to provide additional major food
        resources to other countries? Should they be nationally or
        internationally controlled?

--   On what basis should such food resources then be provided?
        Would food be considered an instrument of national power?
        Will we be forced to make choices as to whom we can
        reasonably assist, and if so, should population efforts be a
        criterion for such assistance?

--   Is the U.S. prepared to accept food rationing to help people
        who can't/won't control their population growth?

--   Should the U.S. seek to change its own food consumption
        patterns toward more efficient uses of protein?

--   Are mandatory population control measures appropriate for
        the U.S. and/or for others?

--   Should the U.S. initiate a major research effort to address
        the growing problems of fresh water supply, ecological
        damage, and adverse climate?

While definitive answers to those questions are not possible in this study given its time limitations and its implications for domestic policy, nevertheless they are needed if one accepts the drastic and persistent character of the population growth problem. Should the choice be made that the recommendations and the options given below are not adequate to meet this problem, consideration should be given to a further study and additional action in this field as outlined above.

Conclusion

The overall strategy above provides a general approach through which the difficulties and dangers of population growth and related problems can be approached in a balanced and comprehensive basis. No single effort will do the job. Only a concerted and major effort in a number of carefully selected directions can provide the hope of success in reducing population growth and its unwanted dangers to world economic will-being and political stability. There are no "quick-fixes" in this field.

Below are specific program recommendations which are designed to implement this strategy. Some will require few new resources; many call for major efforts and significant new resources. We cannot simply buy population growth moderation for nearly 4 billion people "on the cheap".

II. - <u>Action to Create Conditions for Fertility Decline: Population and a Development Assistance Strategy</u>
    A.   <u>General Strategy and Resource Allocations for AID Assistance</u>
           <u>Discussion:</u>

        1. <u>Past Program Actions</u>

Since inception of the program in 1965, AID has obligated nearly $625 million for population activities. These funds have been used primarily to (1) draw attention to the population problem, (2) encourage multilateral and other donor support for the world wide population effort, and (3) help create and maintain the means for attacking the problem, including the development of LDC capabilities to do so.

In pursuing these objectives, AID's population resources were focussed on areas of need where actions was feasible and likely to be effective. AID has provided assistance to population programs in some 70 LDCs, on a bilateral basis and/or indirectly through private organizations and other channels. AID currently provides bilateral assistance to 36 of these countries. State and AID played an important role in establishing the United Nations Fund for Population Activities (UNFPA) to spearhead multilateral effort in population as a complement to the bilateral actions of AID and other donor countries. Since the Fund's establishment, AID has been the largest single contributor. Moreover, with assistance from AID a number of private family planning organizations (e.g., Pathfinder Fund, International Planned Parenthood Foundation, Population Council) have significantly expanded their worldwide population programs. Such organizations are still the main supporters of family planning action in many developing countries.

AID actions have been a major catalyst in stimulating the flow of funds into LDC population programs - from almost nothing ten years ago, the amounts being spent from all sources in 1974 for programs in the developing countries of Africa, Latin America, and Asia (excluding China) will total between $400 and $500 million. About half of this will be contributed by the developed countries bilaterally or through multilateral agencies, and the balance will come from the budgets of the developing countries themselves. AID's contribution is about one-quarter of the total - AID obligated $112.4 million for population programs in FY 1974 and plans for FY 1975 program of $137.5 million.

While world resources for population activities will continue to grow, they are unlikely to expand as rapidly as needed. (<u>One rough</u> estimate is that five times the current amount, or about $2.5 billion in <u>constant dollars</u>, will be required annually by 1985 to provide the 2.5 billion people in the developing world, excluding China, with full-scale family planning programs). In view of these limited resources AID's efforts (in both fiscal and manpower terms) and through its leadership the efforts of others, must be focused to the extent possible on high priority needs in countries where the population problem is the most acute. Accordingly, AID last year began a process of developing geographic and functional program priorities for use in allocating funds and staff, and in arranging and adjusting divisions of labor with other donors and organizations active in the worldwide population effort. Although this study has not yet been completed, a general outline of a U.S. population assistance strategy can be developed from the results of the priorities studied to date. The geographic and functional parameters of the strategy are discussed under 2. and 3. below. The implications for population resource allocations are presented under 4.

2. Geographic Priorities in U.S. Population Assistance

The U.S. strategy should be to encourage and support, through bilateral, multilateral and other channels, constructive actions to lower fertility rates in selected developing countries. Within this overall strategy and in view of funding and manpower limitations, the U.S. should emphasize assistance to those countries where the population problem is the most serious.

There are three major factors to consider in judging the seriousness of the problem:

-- The first is the country's contribution to the world's population problem, which is determined by the size of its population, its population growth rate, and its progress in the "demographic transition" from high birth and high death rates to low ones.

-- The second is the extent to which population growth impinges on the country's economic development and its financial capacity to cope with its population problem.

-- The third factor is the extent to which an imbalance between growing numbers of people and a country's capability to handle the problem could lead to serious instability, international tensions, or conflicts. Although many countries may experience adverse consequences from such imbalances, the trouble making regional or international conditions might not be as serious in some places as they are in others.

Based on the first two criteria, AID has developed a preliminary rank ordering of nearly 100 developing countries which, after review and refinement, will be used as a guide in AID's own funding and manpower resource allocations and in encouraging action through AID leadership efforts on the part of other population assistance instrumentalities. Applying these three criteria to this rank ordering, there are 13 countries where we currently judge the problem and risks to be the most serious. They are: Bangladesh, India, Pakistan, Indonesia, Philippines, Thailand, Egypt, Turkey, Ethiopia, Nigeria, Brazil, Mexico, and Colombia. Out of a total 67 million worldwide increase in population in 1972 these countries contributed about 45%. These countries range from those with virtually no government interest in family planning to those with active government family planning programs which require and would welcome enlarged technical and financial assistance.

These countries should be given the highest priority within AID's population program in terms of resource allocations and/or leadership efforts to encourage action by other donors and organizations. The form and content of our assistance or leadership efforts would vary from country-to-country (as discussed in 3. below), depending on each country's needs, its receptivity to various forms of assistance, its capability to finance needed actions, the effectiveness with which funds can be used, and current or adjusted divisions of labour among the other donors and organizations providing population assistance to the country. AID's population actions would also need to be consistent with the overall U.S. development policy toward each country.

While the countries cited above would be given highest priority, other countries would not be ignored. AID would provide population assistance and/or undertake leadership efforts with respect to other countries to the extent that the availability of funds and staff permits, taking account of such factors as: a country's placement in AID's priority listing of LDCs; its potential impact on domestic unrest and international frictions (which can apply to small as well as large countries); its significance as a test or demonstration case; and opportunities for expenditures that appear particularly cost-effective (e.g. its has been suggested that there may be particularly cost-effective opportunities for supporting family planning to reduce the lag between mortality and fertility declines in countries where death rates are still declining rapidly).

3.   Mode and Content of U.S. Population Assistance

In moving from geographic emphases to strategies for the mode and functional content of population assistance to both the higher and lower priority countries which are to be assisted, various factors need to be considered: (1) the extent of a country's understanding of its population problem and interest in responding to it; (2) the specific actions needed to cope with the problem; (3) the country's need for external financial assistance to deal with the problem; and (4) its receptivity to various forms of assistance.

Some of the countries in the high priority group cited above (e. g. Bangladesh, Pakistan, Indonesia, Philippines, Thailand) and some lower priority countries have recognized that rapid population growth is a problem, are taking actions of their own to deal with it, and are receptive to assistance from the U.S. (through bilateral or central AID funding) and other donors, as well as to multilateral support for their efforts. In these cases AID should continue to provide such assistance based on each country's functional needs, the effectiveness with which funds can be used in these areas, and current or adjusted divisions of labour among other donors and organizations providing assistance to the country. Furthermore, our assistance strategies for these countries should consider their capabilities to finance needed population actions. Countries which have relatively large surpluses of export earning and foreign exchange reserves are unlikely to require large- scale   external financial assistance and should be encouraged to finance their own commodity imports as well as local costs. In such cases our strategy should be to concentrate on needed technical assistance and on attempting to play a catalytic role in encouraging better programs and additional host country financing for dealing with the population problem.

In other high and lower priority countries U.S. assistance is limited either by the nature of political or diplomatic relations with those countries (e.g. India, Egypt), or by the lack of strong government interest in population reduction programs (e.g. Nigeria, Ethiopia, Mexico, Brazil). In such cases, external technical and financial assistance, if desired by the countries, would have to come from other donors and/or from private and international organizations (many of which receive contributions from AID). The USG would, however, maintain an interest (e.g. through Embassies) in such countries' population problems and programs (if any) to reduce population growth rates. Moreover, particularly in the case of high priority countries to which U.S. population assistance is now limited for one reason or another, we should be alert to opportunities for expanding our assistance efforts and for demonstrating to their leaders the consequences of rapid population growth and the benefits of actions to reduce fertility.

In countries to which other forms of U.S. assistance are provided but not population assistance, AID will monitor progress toward achievement of development objectives, taking into account the extent to which these are hindered by rapid population growth, and will look for opportunities to encourage initiation of or improvement in population policies and programs.

In addition, the U.S. strategy should support general activities capable of achieving major breakthroughs in key problems which hinder attainment of fertility control objectives. For example, the development of more effective, simpler contraceptive methods through big-medical research will benefit all countries which face the problem of rapid population growth; improvements in methods for measuring demographic changes will assist a number of LDCs in determining current population growth rates and evaluating the impact over time of population/family planning activities.

4. Resource Allocations for U.S. Population Assistance

AID funds obligated for population/family planning assistance rose steadily since inception of the program ($10 million in the FY 1965-67 period) to nearly $125 million in FY 1972. In FY 1973, however, funds available for population remained at the $125 million level; in FY 1974 they actually declined slightly, to $112.5 million because of a ceiling on population obligations inserted in the legislation by the House Appropriations Committee. With this plateau in AID population obligations, worldwide resources have not been adequate to meet all identified, sensible funding needs, and we therefore see opportunities for significant expansion of the program.

Some major actions in the area of creating conditions for fertility decline, as described in Section JIB, can be funded from AID resources available for the sectors in question (e.g., education, agriculture). Other actions come under the purview of population ("Title X") funds. In this latter category, increases in projected budget requests to the Congress on the order of $35-50 million annually through FY 1980 -- above the $137.5 million requested by FY 1975 -- appear appropriate at this time. Such increases must be accompanied by expanding contributions to the worldwide population effort from other donors and organizations and from the LDCs themselves, if significant progress is to be made. The USG should take advantage of appropriate opportunities to stimulate such contributions from others.

Title X Funding for Population

Year	Amount ($ million)
FY 1972 - Actual Obligations	123.3
FY 1973 - Actual Obligations	125.6
FY 1974 - Actual Obligations	112.4
FY 1975 - Request to Congress	137.5
FY 1976 - Projection	170
FY 1977 - Projection	210
FY 1978 - Projection	250
FY 1979 - Projection	300
FY 1980 - Projection	350

These Title X funding projections for FY 1976-80 are general magnitudes based on preliminary estimates of expansion or initiation of population programs in developing countries and growing requirements for outside assistance as discussed in greater detail in other sections of this paper. These estimates contemplated very substantial increases in self-help and assistance from other donor countries.

Our objective should be to assure that developing countries make family planning information, educational and means available to all their peoples by 1980. Our efforts should include:

-- Increased A.I.D. bilateral and centrally-funded programs, consistent with the geographic priorities cited above.

-- Expanded contributions to multilateral and private organizations that can work effectively in the population area.

-- Further research on the relative impact of various socio-economic factors on desired family size, and experimental efforts to test the feasibility of larger-scale efforts to affect some of these factors.

-- Additional big-medical research to improve the existing means of fertility control and to develop new ones which are safe, effective, inexpensive, and attractive to both men and women.

-- Innovative approaches to providing family planning services, such as the utilization of commercial channels for distribution of contraceptives, and the development of low-cost systems for delivering effective health and family planning services to the 85% of LDC populations not now reached by such services.

-- Expanded efforts to increase the awareness of LDC leaders and publics regarding the consequences of rapid population growth and to stimulate further LDC commitment to actions to reduce fertility.

We believe expansions in the range of 35-50 million annually over the next five years are realistic, in light of potential LDC needs and prospects for increased contributions from other population assistance instrumentalities, as well as constraints on the speed with which AID (and other donors) population funds can be expanded and effectively utilized. These include negative or ambivalent host government attitudes toward population reduction programs; the need for complementary financial and manpower inputs by recipient governments, which must come at the expense of other programs they consider to be high priority; and the need to assure that new projects involve sensible, effective actions that are likely to reduce fertility. We must avoid inadequately planned or implemented programs that lead to extremely high costs per acceptor. In effect, we are closer to "absorptive capacity" in terms of year- to-year increases in population programs than we are, for example, in annual expansions in food, fertilizer or generalized resource transfers.

It would be premature to make detailed funding recommendations by countries and functional categories in light of our inability to predict what changes –- such as in host country attitudes to U.S. population assistance and in fertility control technologies –- may occur which would significantly alter funding needs in particular geographic or functional areas. For example, AID is currently precluded from providing bilateral assistance to India and Egypt, two significant countries in the highest priority group, due to the nature of U.S. political and diplomatic relations with these countries. However, if these relationships were to change and bilateral aid could be provided, we would want to consider providing appropriate population assistance to these countries. In other cases, changing U.S. - LDC relationships might preclude further aid to some countries. Factors such as these could both change the mix and affect overall magnitudes of funds needed for population assistance. Therefore, proposed program mixes and funding levels by geographic and functional categories should continue to be examined on an annual basis during the regular USG program and budget review processes which lead to the presentation of funding requests to the Congress.

Recognizing that changing opportunities for action could substantially affect AID's resource requirements for population assistance, we anticipate that, if funds are provided by the Congress at the levels projected, we would be able to cover necessary actions related to the highest priority countries and also those related to lower priority countries, moving reasonably far down the list. At this point, however, AID believes it would not be desirable to make priority judgments on which activities would not be funded if Congress did not provide the levels projected. If cuts were made in these levels we would have to make judgments based on such factors as the priority rankings of countries, then-existing LDC needs, and divisions of labour with other actors in the population assistance area.

If AID's population assistance program is to expand at the general magnitudes cited above, additional direct hire staff will likely be needed. While the expansion in program action would be primarily through grants and contracts with LDC or U.S. institutions, or through contributions to international organizations, increases in direct hire staff would be necessary to review project proposals, monitor their implementation through such instrumentalities, and evaluate their progress against pre-established goals. Specific direct hire manpower requirements should continue to be considered during the annual program and budget reviews, along with details of program mix and funding levels by country and functional category, in order to correlate staffing needs with projected program actions for a particular year.

Recommendations

1. The U.S. strategy should be to encourage and support, through bilateral, multilateral and other channels, constructive action to lower fertility rates in selected developing countries. The U.S. should apply each of the relevant provisions of its World Population Plan of Action and use it to influence and support actions by developing countries.

2. Within this overall strategy, the U.S. should give highest priority, in terms of resource allocation (along with donors) to efforts to encourage assistance from others to those countries cited above where the population problem is most serious, and provide assistance to other countries as funds and staff permit.

3. AID's further development of population program priorities, both geographic and functional, should be consistent with the general strategy discussed above, with the other recommendations of this paper and with the World Population Plan of Action. The strategies should be coordinated with the population activities of other donors countries and agencies using the WPPA as leverage to obtain suitable action.

4. AID's budget requests over the next five years should include a major expansion of bilateral population and family planning programs (as appropriate for each country or region), of functional activities as necessary, and of contributions through multilateral channels, consistent with the general funding magnitudes discussed above. The proposed budgets should emphasize the country and functional priorities outlined in the recommendations of this study and as detailed in AID's geographic and functional strategy papers.

II B. <u>Functional Assistance Programs to Create Conditions for Fertility Decline</u>

    <u>Introduction</u>

        <u>Discussion</u>

It is clear that the availability of contraceptive services and information, important as that is, is not the only element required to address the population problems of the LDCs. Substantial evidence shows that many families in LDCs (especially the poor) consciously prefer to have numerous children for a variety of economic and social reasons. For example, small children can make economic contributions on family farms, children can be important sources of support for old parents where no alternative form of social security exists, and children may be a source of status for women who have few alternatives in male-dominated societies.

The desire for large families diminishes as income rises. Developed countries and the more developed areas in LDCs have lower fertility than less developed areas. Similarly, family planning programs produce more acceptors and have a greater impact on fertility in developed areas than they do in less developed areas. Thus, investments in development are important in lowering fertility rates. We know that the major socio-economic determinants of fertility are strongly interrelated. A change in any one of them is likely to produce a change in the others as well. Clearly development per se is a powerful determinant of fertility. However, since it is unlikely that most LDCs will develop sufficiently during the next 25-30 years, it is crucial to identify those sectors that most directly and powerfully affect fertility.

In this context, population should be viewed as a variable which interacts, to differing degrees, with a wide range of development programs, and the U.S. strategy should continue to stress the importance of taking population into account in "non-family planning" activities. This is particularly important with the increasing focus in the U.S. development program on food and nutrition, health and population, and education and human resources; assistance programs have less chance of success as long as the numbers to be fed, educated, and employed are increasing rapidly.

Thus, to assist in achieving LDC fertility reduction, not only should family planning be high up on the priority list for U.S. foreign assistance, but high priority in allocation of funds should be given to programs in other sectors that contribute in a cost-effective manner in reduction in population growth.

There is a growing, but still quite small, body of research to determine the socio-economic aspects of development that most directly and powerfully affect fertility. Although the limited analysis to date cannot be considered definitive, there is general agreement that the five following factors (in addition to increases in per capita income) tend to be strongly associated with fertility declines: education, especially the education of women; reductions in infant mortality; wage employment opportunities for women; social security and other substitutes for the economic value of children; and relative equality in income distribution and rural development. There are a number of other factors identified from research, historical analysis, and experimentation that also affect fertility, including delaying the average age of marriage, and direct payments (financial incentive) to family planning acceptors.

There are, however, number of questions which must be addressed before one can move from identification of factors associated with fertility decline to large-scale programs that will induce fertility decline in a cost-effective manner. For example, in the case of female education, we need to consider such questions as: did the female education cause fertility to decline or did the development process in some situations cause parents both to see less economic need for large families and to indulge in the "luxury" of educating their daughters? If more female education does in fact cause fertility declines, will poor high-fertility parents see much advantage in sending their daughters to school? If so, how much does it cost to educate a girl to the point where her fertility will be reduced (which occurs at about the fourth-grade level)? What specific programs in female education are most cost-effective (e.g., primary school, non-formal literacy training, or vocational or pre-vocational training)? What, in rough quantitative terms, are the non-population benefits of an additional dollar spent on female education in a given situation in comparison to other non-population investment alternatives? What are the population benefits of a dollar spent on female education in comparison with other population-related investments, such as in contraceptive supplies or in maternal and child health care systems? And finally, what is the total population plus non-population benefit of investment in a given specific program in female education in comparison with the total population plus non-population benefits of alternate feasible investment opportunities?

As a recent research proposal from Harvard's Department of Population Studies puts this problem: "Recent studies have identified more specific factors underlying fertility declines, especially, the spread of educational attainment and the broadening of nontraditional roles for women. In situations of rapid population growth, however, these run counter to powerful market forces. Even when efforts are made to provide educational opportunities for most of the school age population, low levels of development and restricted employment opportunities for academically educated youth lead to high dropout rates and non-attendance..."

Fortunately, the situation is by no means as ambiguous for all of the likely factors affecting fertility. For example, laws that raise the minimum marriage age, where politically feasible and at least partially enforceable, can over time have a modest effect on fertility at negligible cost. Similarly, there have been some controversial, but remarkably successful, experiments in India in which financial incentives, along with other motivational devices, were used to get large numbers of men to accept vasectomies. In addition, there appear to be some major activities, such as programs aimed to improve the productive capacity of the rural poor, which can be well justified even without reference to population benefits, but which appear to have major population benefits as well.

The strategy suggested by the above considerations is that the volume and type of programs aimed at the "determinants of fertility" should be directly related to our estimate of the total benefits (including non-population benefits) of a dollar invested in a given proposed program and to our confidence in the reliability of that estimate. There is room for honest disagreement among researchers and policy-makers about the benefits, or feasibility, of a given program. Hopefully, over time, with more research, experimentation and evaluation, areas of disagreement and ambiguity will be clarified, and donors and recipients will have better information both on what policies and programs tend to work under what circumstances and how to go about analysing a given country situation to find the best feasible steps that should be taken.

Recommendations:

1. AID should implement the strategy set out in the World Population Plan of Action, especially paragraphs 31 and 32 and Section I ("Introduction - a U.S. Global Population Strategy") above, which calls for high priority in funding to three categories of programs in areas affecting fertility (family- size) decisions:

> a. Operational programs where there is proven cost- effectiveness, generally where there are also significant benefits for non-population objectives;
>
> b. Experimental programs where research indicates close relationships to fertility reduction but cost-effectiveness has not yet been demonstrated in terms of specific steps to be taken (i.e., program design); and
>
> c. Research and evaluation on the relative impact on desired family size of the socio-economic determinants of fertility, and on what policy scope exists for affecting these determinants.

2. Research, experimentation and evaluation of ongoing programs should focus on answering the questions (such as those raised above, relating to female education) that determine what steps can and should be taken in other sectors that will in a cost-effective manner speed up the rate of fertility decline. In addition to the five areas discussed in Section II. B 1-5 below, the research should also cover the full range of factors affecting fertility, such as laws and norms respecting age of marriage, and financial incentives. Work of this sort should be undertaken in individual key countries to determine the motivational factors required there to develop a preference for small family size. High priority must be given to testing feasibility and replicability on a wide scale.

3. AID should encourage other donors in LDC governments to carry out parallel strategies of research, experimentation, and (cost-effective well-evaluated) large-scale operations programs on factors affecting fertility. Work in this area should be coordinated, and results shared.

4. AID should help develop capacity in a few existing U.S. and LDC institutions to serve as major centers for research and policy development in the areas of fertility-affecting social or economic measures, direct incentives, household behavior research, and evaluation techniques for motivational approaches. The centers should provide technical assistance, serve as

a forum for discussion, and generally provide the "critical mass" of effort and visibility which has been lacking in this area to date. Emphasis should be given to maximum involvement of LDC institutions and individuals.

The following sections discuss research experimental and operational programs to be undertaken in the five promising areas mentioned above.

1. <u>Providing Minimal Levels of Education, Especially for Women</u>

<u>Discussion</u>

There is fairly convincing evidence that female education especially of 4th grade and above correlates strongly with reduced desired family size, although it is unclear the extent to which the female education causes reductions in desired family size or whether it is a faster pace of development which leads both to increased demand for female education and to reduction in desired family size. There is also a relatively widely held theory -- though not statistically validated -- that improved levels of literacy contribute to reduction in desired family size both through greater knowledge of family planning information and increasing motivational factors related to reductions in family size. Unfortunately, AID's experience with mass literacy programs over the past 15 years has yielded the sobering conclusion that such programs generally failed (i.e. were not cost-effective) unless the population sees practical benefits to themselves from learning how to read -- e.g., a requirement for literacy to acquire easier access to information about new agricultural technologies or to jobs that require literacy.

Now, however, AID has recently revised its education strategy, in line with the mandate of its legislation, to place emphasis on the spread of education to poor people, particularly in rural areas, and relatively less on higher levels of education. This approach is focused on use of formal and "non-formal" education (i.e., organized education outside the schoolroom setting) to assist in meeting the human resource requirements of the development process, including such things as rural literacy programs aimed at agriculture, family planning, or other development goals.

<u>Recommendations</u>

1. Integrated basic education (including applied literacy) and family planning programs should be developed whenever they appear to be effective, of high priority, and acceptable to the individual country. AID should continue its emphasis on basic education, for women as well as men.

2. A major effort should be made in LDCs seeking to reduce birth rates to assure at least an elementary school education for virtually all children, girls as well as boys, as soon as the country can afford it (which would be quite soon for all but the poorest countries). Simplified, practical education programs should be developed. These programs should, where feasible, include specific curricula to motivate the next generation toward a two-child family average to

assure that level of fertility in two or three decades. AID should encourage and respond to requests for assistance in extending basic education and in introducing family planning into curricula. Expenditures for such emphasis on increased practical education should come from general AID funds, not population funds.

2. Reducing Infant and Child Mortality

Discussion:

High infant and child mortality rates, evident in many developing countries, lead parents to be concerned about the number of their children who are likely to survive. Parents may over compensate for possible child losses by having additional children. Research to date clearly indicates not only that high fertility and high birth rates are closely correlated but that in most circumstances low net population growth rates can only be achieved when child mortality is low as well. Policies and programs which significantly reduce infant and child mortality below present levels will lead couples to have fewer children. However, we must recognize that there is a lag of at least several years before parents (and cultures and subcultures) become confident that their children are more likely to survive and to adjust their fertility behaviour accordingly.

Considerable reduction in infant and child mortality is possible through improvement in nutrition, inoculations against diseases, and other public health measures if means can be devised for extending such services to neglected LDC populations on a low-cost basis. It often makes sense to combine such activities with family planning services in integrated delivery systems in order to maximize the use of scarce LDC financial and health manpower resources (See Section IV). In addition, providing selected health care for both mothers and their children can enhance the acceptability of family planning by showing concern for the whole condition of the mother and her children and not just for the single factor of fertility.

The two major cost-effective problems in maternal-child health care are that clinical health care delivery systems have not in the past accounted for much of the reduction in infant mortality and that, as in the U.S., local medical communities tend to favor relatively expensive quality health care, even at the cost of leaving large numbers of people (in the LDC's generally over two-thirds of the people) virtually uncovered by modern health services.

Although we do not have all the answers on how to develop inexpensive, integrated delivery systems, we need to proceed with operational programs to respond to ODC requests if they are likely to be cost-effective based on experience to date, and to experiment on a large scale with innovative ways of tackling the outstanding problems. Evaluation mechanisms for measuring the impact of various courses of action are an essential part of this effort in order to provide feedback for current and future projects and to improve the state of the art in this field.

Currently, efforts to develop low-cost health and family planning services for neglected populations in the LDC's are impeded because of the lack of international commitment and resources to the health side. For example:

CONFIDENTIAL

A. The World Bank could supply low interest credits to LDCs for the development of low-cost health-related services to neglected populations but has not yet made a policy decision to do so. The Bank has a population and health program and the program's leaders have been quite sympathetic with the above objective. The Bank's staff has prepared a policy paper on this subject for the Board but prospects for it are not good. Currently, the paper will be discussed by the Bank Board at its November 1974 meeting. Apparently there is some reticence within the Bank's Board and in parts of the staff about making a strong initiative in this area. In part, the Bank argues that there are not proven models of effective, low-cost health systems in which the Bank can invest. The Bank also argues that other sectors such as agriculture, should receive higher priority in the competition for scarce resources. In addition, arguments are made in some quarters of the Bank that the Bank ought to restrict itself to "hard loan projects" and not get into the "soft" area.

A current reading from the Bank's staff suggests that unless there is some change in the thinking of the Bank Board, the Bank's policy will be simply to keep trying to help in the population and health areas but not to take any large initiative in the low-cost delivery system area.

The Bank stance is regrettable because the Bank could play a very useful role in this area helping to fund low-cost physical structures and other elements of low-cost health systems, including rural health clinics where needed. It could also help in providing low-cost loans for training, and in seeking and testing new approaches to reaching those who do not now have access to health and family planning services. This would not be at all inconsistent with our and the Bank's frankly admitting that we do not have all the "answer" or cost- effective models for low-cost health delivery systems. Rather they, we and other donors could work together on experimentally oriented, operational programs to develop models for the wide variety of situations faced by LDCs.

Involvement of the Bank in this area would open up new possibilities for collaboration. Grant funds, whether from the U.S. or UNFPA, could be used to handle the parts of the action that require short lead times such as immediate provision of supplies, certain kinds of training and rapid deployment of technical assistance. Simultaneously, for parts of the action that require longer lead times, such as building clinics, World Bank loans could be employed. The Bank's lending processes could be synchronized to bring such building activity to a readiness condition at the time the training programs have moved along far enough to permit manning of the facilities. The emphasis should be on meeting low-cost rather than high-cost infrastructure requirements.

Obviously, in addition to building, we assume the Bank could fund other local-cost elements of expansion of health systems such as longer-term training programs.

AID is currently trying to work out improved consultation procedures with the Bank staff in the hope of achieving better collaborative efforts within the Bank's current commitment of resources in the population and health areas. With a greater commitment of Bank resources and improved consultation with AID and UNFPA, a much greater dent could be made on the overall problem.

B. The World Health Organization (WHO) and its counterpart for Latin America, the Pan American Health Organization (PAHO), currently provide technical assistance in the development and implementation of health projects which are in turn financed by international funding mechanisms such as UNDP and the International Financial Institutions. However, funds available for health actions through these organizations are limited at present. Higher priority by the international funding agencies to health actions could expand the opportunities for useful collaborations among donor institutions and countries to develop low-cost integrated health and family planning delivery systems for LDC populations that do not now have access to such services.

Recommendations:

The U.S. should encourage heightened international interest in and commitment of resources to developing delivery mechanisms for providing integrated health and family planning services to neglected populations at costs which host countries can support within a reasonable period of time. Efforts should include:

1. Encouraging the World Bank and other international funding mechanisms, through the U.S. representatives on the boards of these organizations, to take a broader initiative in the development of inexpensive service delivery mechanisms in countries wishing to expand such systems.

2. Indicating U.S. willingness (as the U.S. did at the World Population Conference) to join with other donors and organizations to encourage and support further action by LDC governments and other institutions in the low- cost delivery systems area.

A. As offered at Bucharest, the U.S. should join donor countries, WHO, UNFPA, UNICEF and the World Bank to create a consortium to offer assistance to the more needy developing countries to establish their own low-cost preventive and curative public health systems reaching into all areas of their countries and capable of national support within a reasonable period. Such systems would include family planning services as an ordinary part of their overall services.

B. The WHO should be asked to take the leadership in such an arrangement and is ready to do so. Apparently at least half of the potential donor countries and the EEC's technical assistance program are favourably inclined. So is the UNFPA and UNICEF. The U.S., through its representation on the World Bank Board, should encourage a broader World Bank initiative in this field, particularly to assist in the development of inexpensive, basic health service infrastructures in countries wishing to undertake the development of such systems.

3. Expanding Wage Employment Opportunities, Especially for Women

Discussion

Employment is the key to access to income, which opens the way to improved health, education, nutrition, and reduced family size. Reliable job opportunities enable parents to limit their family size and invest in the welfare of the children they have.

The status and utilization of women in LDC societies is particularly important in reducing family size. For women, employment outside the home offers an alternative to early marriage and childbearing, and an incentive to have fewer children after marriage. The woman who must stay home to take care of her children must forego the income she could earn outside the home. Research indicates that female wage employment outside the home is related to fertility reduction. Programs to increase the women's labour force participation must, however, take account of the overall demand for labour; this would be a particular problem in occupations where there is already widespread unemployment among males. But other occupations where women have a comparative advantage can be encouraged.

Improving the legal and social status of women gives women a greater voice in decision-making about their lives, including family size, and can provide alternative opportunities to childbearing, thereby reducing the benefits of having children.

The U.S. Delegation to the Bucharest Conference emphasized the importance of improving the general status of women and of developing employment opportunities for women outside the home and off the farm. It was joined by all countries in adopting a strong statement on this vital issue. See Chapter VI for a fuller discussion of the conference.

Recommendations:

1. AID should communicate with and seek opportunities to assist national economic development programs to increase the role of women in the development process.

2. AID should review its education/training programs (such as U.S. participant training, in-country and third-country training) to see that such activities provide equal access to women.

3. AID should enlarge pre-vocational and vocational training to involve women more directly in learning skills which can enhance their income and status in the community (e.g. paramedical skills related to provision of family planning services).

4. AID should encourage the development and placement of LDC women as decision-makers in development programs, particularly those programs designed to increase the role of women as producers of goods and services, and otherwise to improve women's welfare (e.g. national credit and finance programs, and national health and family planning programs).

5. AID should encourage, where possible, women's active participation in the labour movement in order to promote equal pay for equal work, equal benefits, and equal employment opportunities.

6. AID should continue to review its programs and projects for their impact on LDC women, and adjust them as necessary to foster greater participation of women - particularly those in the lowest classes - in the development process.

4. Developing Alternatives to the Social Security Role Provided By Children to Aging Parents

Discussion:

In most LDCs the almost total absence of government or other institutional forms of social security for old people forces dependence on children for old age survival. The need for such support appears to be one of the important motivations for having numerous children. Several proposals have been made, and a few pilot experiments are being conducted, to test the impact of financial incentives designed to provide old age support (or, more tangentially, to increase the earning power of fewer children by financing education costs parents would otherwise bear). Proposals have been made for son-insurance (provided to the parents if they have no more than three children), and for deferred payments of retirement benefits (again tied to specified limits on family size), where the payment of the incentive is delayed. The intent is not only to tie the incentive to actual fertility, but to impose the financial cost on the government or private sector entity only after the benefits of the avoided births have accrued to the economy and the financing entity. Schemes of varying administrative complexity have been developed to take account of management problems in LDCs. The economic and equity core of these long-term incentive proposals is simple: the government offers to return to the contracting couple a portion of the economic dividend they generate by avoiding births, as a direct trade-off for the personal financial benefits they forego by having fewer children.

Further research and experimentation in this area needs to take into account the impact of growing urbanization in LDCs on traditional rural values and outlooks such as the desire for children as old-age insurance.

Recommendation:

AID should take a positive stance with respect to exploration of social security type incentives as described above. AID should encourage governments to consider such measures, and should provide financial and technical assistance where appropriate. The recommendation made earlier to establish an "intermediary" institutional capacity which could provide LDC governments with substantial assistance in this area, among several areas on the "demand" side of the problem, would add considerably to AID's ability to carry out this recommendation.

5. Pursuing Development Strategies that Skew Income Growth Toward the Poor, Especially Rural Development Focussing on Rural Poverty

Income distribution and rural development: The higher a family's income, the fewer children it will probably have, except at the very top of the income scale. Similarly, the more evenly distributed the income in a society, the lower the overall fertility rate seems to be since better income distribution means that the poor, who have the highest fertility, have higher income. Thus a development strategy which emphasizes the rural poor, who are the largest and poorest group in most LDCs would be providing income increases to those with the highest fertility levels. No LDC is likely to achieve population stability unless the rural poor participate in income increases and fertility declines.

Agriculture and rural development is already, along with population, the US. Government's highest priority in provision of assistance to LDCs. For FY 1975, about 60% of the $1.13 billion AID requested in the five functional areas of the foreign assistance legislation is in agriculture and rural development. The $255 million increase in the FY 1975 level authorized in the two year FY 1974 authorization bill is virtually all for agriculture and rural development.

AID's primary goal in agriculture and rural development is concentration in   food output and increases in the rural quality of life; the major strategy element is concentration on increasing the output of small farmers, through assistance in provision of improved technologies, agricultural inputs, institutional supports, etc.

This strategy addresses three U.S. interests: First, it increases agricultural output in the LDCs, and speeds up the average pace of their development, which, as has been noted, leads to increased acceptance of family planning. Second, the emphasis on small farmers and other elements of the rural poor spreads the benefits of development as broadly as is feasible among lower income groups. As noted above spreading the benefits of development to the poor, who tend to have the highest fertility rates, is an important step in getting them to reduce their family size. In addition, the concentration on small farmer production (vs., for example, highly mechanized, large-scale agriculture) can increase on and off farm rural job opportunities and decrease the flow to the cities. While fertility levels in rural areas are higher than in the cities, continued rapid migration into the cities at levels greater than the cities' job markets or services can sustain adds an important destabilizing element to development efforts and goals of many countries. Indeed, urban areas in some LDCs are already the scene of urban unrest and high crime rates.

Recommendation

AID should continue its efforts to focus not just on agriculture and rural development but specifically on small farmers and on labour-intensive means of stimulating agricultural output and on other aspects of improving the quality of life of the rural poor, so that agriculture and rural development assistance, in addition to its importance for increased food production and other purposes, can have maximum impact on reducing population growth.

6. Concentration on Education and Indoctrination of The Rising Generation of Children Regarding the Desirability of Smaller Family Size

Discussion:

Present efforts at reducing birth rates in LDCs, including AID and UNFPA assistance, are directed largely at adults now in their reproductive years. Only nominal attention is given to population education or sex education in schools and in most countries none is given in the very early grades which are the only attainment of 2/3-3/4 of the children. It should be obvious, however, that efforts at birth control directed toward adults will with even maximum success result in acceptance of contraception for the reduction of births only to the level of the desired family size — which knowledge, attitude and practice studies in many countries indicate is an average of four or more children.

The great necessity is to convince the masses of the population that it is to their individual and national interest to have, on the average, only three and then only two children. There is little likelihood that this result can be accomplished very widely against the background of the cultural heritage of today's adults, even the young adults, among the masses in most LDCs. Without diminishing in any way the effort to reach these adults, the obvious increased focus of attention should be to change the attitudes of the next generation, those who are now in elementary school or younger. If this could be done, it would indeed be possible to attain a level of fertility approaching replacement in 20 years and actually reaching it in 30.

Because a large percentage of children from high-fertility, low income groups do not attend school, it will be necessary to develop means to reach them for this and other educational purposes through informal educational programs. As the discussion earlier of the determinants of family size (fertility) pointed out, it is also important to make significant progress in other areas, such as better health care and improvements in income distribution, before desired family size can be expected to fall sharply. If it makes economic sense for poor parents to have large families twenty years from now, there is no evidence as to whether population education or indoctrination will have sufficient impact alone to dissuade them.

Recommendation

1. That U.S. agencies stress the importance of education of the next generation of parents, starting in elementary schools, toward a two-child family ideal.

2. That AID stimulate specific efforts to develop means of educating children of elementary school age to the ideal of the two-child family and that UNESCO be asked to take the lead through formal and informal education.

General Recommendation for UN Agencies

As to each of the above six categories State and AID should make specific efforts to have the relevant UN agency, WHO, ILO, FAO, UNESCO, UNICEF, and the UNFPA take its proper role of leadership in the UN family with increased program effort, citing the world Population Plan of Action.

II. C. Food for Peace Program and Population

Discussion:

One of the most fundamental aspects of the impact of population growth on the political and economic well-being of the globe is its relationship to food. Here the problem of the interrelationship of population, national resources, environment, productivity and political and economic stability come together when shortages of this basic human need occur.

USDA projections indicate that the quantity of grain imports needed by the LDCs in the 1980s will grow significantly, both in overall and per capita terms. In addition, these countries will face year-to-year fluctuations weather and other factors.

This is not to say that the LDCs need face starvation in the next two decades, for the same projections indicate an even greater increase in production of grains in the developed nations. It should be pointed out, however, that these projections assume that such major problems as the vast increase in the need for fresh water, the ecological effects of the vast increase in the application of fertilizer, pesticides, and irrigation, and the apparent adverse trend in the global climate, are solved. At present, there are no solutions to these problems in sight.

The major challenge will be to increase food production in the LDCs themselves and to liberalize the system in which grain is transferred commercially from producer to consumer countries. We also see food aid as an important way of meeting part of the chronic shortfall and emergency needs caused by year-to-year variation at least through the end of this decade. Many outside experts predict just such difficulties even if major efforts are undertaken to expand world agricultural output, especially in the LDCs themselves but also in the U.S. and in other major feed grain producers. In the longer run, LDCs must both decrease population growth and increase agricultural production significantly. At some point the "excess capacity" of the food exporting countries will run out. Some countries have already moved from a net food exporter to a net importer of food.

There are major inter-agency studies now progressing in the food area and this report cannot go deeply into this field. It can only point to serious problems as they relate to population and suggest minimum requirements and goals in the food area.

In particular, we believe that population growth may have very serious negative consequences on food production in the LDCs including over-expectations of the capacity of the land to produce, downgrading the ecological economics of marginal areas, and over-harvesting the seas. All of these conditions may affect the viability of the world's economy and thereby its prospects for peace and security.

Recommendations:

Since NSC/CIEP studies are already underway we refer the reader to them. However the following, we believe, are minimum requirements for any strategy which wishes to avoid instability and conflict brought on by population growth and food scarcity:

(1) High priority for U.S. bilateral and multilateral LDC Agricultural Assistance; including efforts by the LDCs to improve food production and distribution with necessary institutional adjustments and economic policies to stimulate efficient production. This must include a significant increase in financial and technical aid to promote more efficient production and distribution in the LDCs.

(2) Development of national food stocks *(including those needed for emergency relief -) within an internationally agreed framework sufficient to provide an adequate level of world food security;

(3) Expansion of production of the input elements of food production (i.e., fertilizer, availability of water and high yield seed stocks) and increased incentives for expanded agricultural productivity. In this context a reduction n the real cost of energy (especially fuel) either through expansion in availability through new sources or decline in the relative price of oil or both would be of great importance;

(4) Significant expansion of U.S. and other producer country food crops within the context of a liberalized and efficient world trade system that will assure food availability to the LDCs in case of severe shortage. New international trade arrangements for agricultural products, open enough to permit maximum production by efficient producers and flexible enough to dampen wide price fluctuations in years when weather conditions result in either significant shortfalls or surpluses. We believe this objective can be achieved by trade liberalization and an internationally coordinated food reserve program without resorting to price-oriented agreements, which have undesirable effects on both production and distribution;

(5) The maintenance of an adequate food aid program with a clearer focus on its use as a means to make up real food deficits, pending the development of their own food resources, in
countries unable to feed themselves rather than as primarily an economic development or foreign policy instrument; and

(6) A strengthened research effort, including long term, to develop new seed and

---

* Department of Agriculture favours U.S. commercial interests holding any national stocks in an international network of stockpiles

farming technologies, primarily to increase yields but also to permit more extensive cultivation techniques, particularly in LDCs.

III. International Organizations and other Multilateral Population Programs

A. UN Organization and Specialized Agencies

Discussion

In the mid-sixties the UN member countries slowly began to agree on a greater involvement of the United Nations in population matters. In 1967 the Secretary-General created a Trust Fund to finance work in the population field. In 1969 the Fund was renamed the United Nations Fund for Population Activities (UNFPA) and placed under the overall supervision of the United Nations Development Program. During this period, also, the mandates of the Specialized Agencies were modified to permit greater involvement by these agencies in population activities.

UNFPA's role was clarified by an ECOSOC resolution in 1973: (a) to build up the knowledge and capacity to respond to the needs in the population and family planning fields; (b) to promote awareness in both developed and developing countries of the social, economic, and environmental implications of population problems; (c) to extend assistance to developing countries; and (d) to promote population programs and to coordinate projects supported by the UNFPA.

Most of the projects financed by UNFPA are implemented with the assistance of organizations of the United Nations system, including the regional Economic Commission, United Nations Children's Fund (UNICEF), International Labour Organization (ILO), Food and Agriculture Organization (FAO), United Nations Educational Scientific and Cultural Organization (UNESCO), the World Health Organization (WHO). Collaborative arrangements have been made with the International Development Association (IDA), an affiliate of the World Bank, and with the World Food Programme.

Increasingly the UNFPA is moving toward comprehensive country programs negotiated directly with governments. This permits the governments to select the implementing (executing) agency which may be a member of the UN system or a non-government organization or company. With the development of the country program approach it is planned to level off UNFPA funding to the specialized agencies.

UNFPA has received $122 million in voluntary contributions from 65 governments, of which $42 million was raised in 1973. The Work Plan of UNFPA for 1974-77 sets a $280 million goal for fund-raising, as follows:

> 1974 - $54 million
> 1975 - $64 million
> 1976 - $76 million
> 1977 - $86 million

Through 1971 the U.S. had contributed approximately half of all the funds contributed to UNFPA. In 1972 we reduced our matching contribution to 48 percent of other donations, and for 1973 we further reduced our contribution to 45%. In 1973 requests for UNFPA assistance had begun to exceed available resources. This trend has accelerated and demand for UNFPA resources is now strongly outrunning supply. Documented need for UNFPA assistance during the years 1974-77 is $350 million, but because the UNFPA could anticipate that only $280 million will be available it has been necessary to phase the balance to at least 1978.

Recommendations:

The U.S. should continue its support of multilateral efforts in the population field by:

a) increasing, subject to congressional appropriation action, the absolute contribution to the UNFPA in light of 1) mounting demands for UNFPA Assistance, 2) improving UNFPA capacity to administer projects, 3) the extent to which UNFPA funding aims at U.S. objectives and will substitute for U.S. funding, 4) the prospect that without increased U.S. contributions the UNFPA will be unable to raise sufficient funds for its budget in 1975 and beyond;

b) initiating or participating in an effort to increase the resources from other donors made available to international agencies that can work effectively in the population area as both to increase overall population efforts and, in the UNFPA, to further reduce the U.S. percentage share of total contributions; and

c) supporting the coordinating role which UNFPA plays among donor and recipient countries, and among UN and other organizations in the population field, including the World Bank.

B.   Encouraging Private Organizations

Discussion

The cooperation of private organizations and groups on a national, regional and world-wide level is essential to the success of a comprehensive population strategy. These groups provide important intellectual contributions and policy support, as well as the delivery of family planning and health services and information. In some countries, the private and voluntary organizations are the only means of providing family planning services and materials.

Recommendations:

AID should continue to provide support to those private U.S. and international organizations whose work contributes to reducing rapid population growth, and to develop with them, where appropriate, geographic and functional divisions of labor in population assistance.

IV.   Provision and Development of Family Planning Services, Information and Technology

In addition to creating the climate for fertility decline, as described in a previous section, it is essential to provide safe and effective techniques for controlling fertility.

There are two main elements in this task: (a) improving the effectiveness of the existing means of fertility control and developing new ones; and (b) developing low-cost systems for the delivery of family planning technologies, information and related services to the 85% of LDC populations not now reached.

Legislation and policies affecting what the U.S. Government does relative to abortion in the above areas is discussed at the end of this section.

A. Research to Improve Fertility Control Technology

Discussion

The effort to reduce population growth requires a variety of birth control methods which are safe, effective, inexpensive and attractive to both men and women. The developing countries in particular need methods which do not require physicians and which are suitable for use in primitive, remote rural areas or urban slums by people with relatively low motivation. Experiences in family planning have clearly demonstrated the crucial impact of improved technology on fertility control.

None of the currently available methods of fertility control is completely effective and free of adverse reactions and objectionable characteristics. The ideal of a contraceptive, perfect in all these respects, may never be realized. A great deal of effort and money will be necessary to improve fertility control methods. The research to achieve this aim can be divided into two categories:

1.   Short-term approaches: These include applied and developmental work which is required to perfect further and evaluate the safety and role of methods demonstrated to be effective in family planning programs in the developing countries.
      Other work is directed toward new methods based on well established knowledge about the physiology of reproduction. Although short term pay-offs are possible, successful development of some methods may take 5 years and up to $15 million for a single method.

2.   Long-term approaches: The limited state of- fundamental knowledge of many reproductive processes requires that a strong research effort of a more basic nature be maintained to elucidate these processes and provide leads for contraceptive development research. For example, new knowledge of

male reproductive processes is needed before research to develop a male "pill" can come to fruition. Costs and duration of the required research are high and difficult to quantify.

With expenditures of about $30 million annually, a broad program of basic and applied big-medical research on human reproduction and contraceptive development is carried out by the Center for Population Research of the National Institute of Child Health and Human Development. The Agency for International Development annually funds about $5 million of principally applied research on new means of fertility control suitable for use in developing countries.

Smaller sums are spent by other agencies of the U.S. Government. Coordination of the federal research effort is facilitated by the activities of the Interagency Committee on Population Research. This committee prepares an annual listing and analyses of all government supported population research programs. The listing is published in the Inventory of Federal Population Research.

A variety of studies have been undertaken by non-governmental experts including the U.S. Commission on Population Growth and the American Future. Most of these studies indicate that the United States effort in population research is insufficient. Opinions differ on how much more can be spent wisely and effectively but an additional $25-50 million annually for bio-medical research constitutes a conservative estimate.

Recommendations:

A stepwise increase over the next 3 years to a total of about $100 million annually for fertility and contraceptive research is recommended. This is an increase of $60 million over the current $40 million expended annually by the major Federal Agencies for biomedical research. Of this increase $40 million would be spent on short-term, goal directed research. The current expenditure of $20 million in long-term approaches consisting largely of basic biomedical research would be doubled. This increased effort would require significantly increased staffing of the federal agencies which support this work. Areas recommended for further research are:

1. Short-term approaches: These approaches include improvement and field testing of existing technology and development of new technology. It is expected that some of these approaches would be ready for use within five years. Specific short term approaches worthy of increased effort are as follows:

    a. Oral contraceptives have become popular and widely used; yet the optimal steroid hormone combinations and doses for LDC populations need further definition. Field studies in several settings are required. Approx. Increased Cost: $3 million annually.

    b. Intra-uterine devices of differing size, shape, and bioactivity should be developed and tested to determine the optimum levels of effectiveness, safety, and acceptability. Approx. Increased Cost: $3 million annually.

    c.   <u>Improved methods for ovulation</u> prediction will be important to those couples who wish to practice rhythm with more assurance of effectiveness than they now have. Approx. Increased Cost: $3 million annually.

    d.   <u>Sterilization of men and women</u> has received wide-spread acceptance in several areas when a simple, quick, and safe procedure is readily available. Female sterilization has been improved by technical advances with laparoscopes, culdoscopes, and greatly simplifies abdominal surgical techniques. Further improvements by the use of tubal clips, trans-cervical approaches, and simpler techniques can be developed. For men several current techniques hold promise but require more refinement and evaluation. Approx. Increased Cost $6 million annually.

    e.   <u>Injectable contraceptives for women</u> which are effective for three months or more and are administered by pare-professionals undoubtedly will be a significant improvement. Currently available methods of this type are limited by their side effects and potential hazards. There are reasons to believe that these problems can be overcome with additional research. Approx. Increased Cost: $5 million annually.

    f.   <u>Leuteolytic and anto-progesterone</u> approaches to fertility control including use of prostaglandins are theoretically attractive but considerable work remains to be done. Approx. Increased Cost: $7 million annually.

    g.   <u>Non-Clinical Methods</u>. Additional research on non-clinical methods including foams, creams, and condoms is needed. These methods can be used without medical supervision. Approx. Increased Cost; $5 million annually.

    h.   <u>Field studies</u>. Clinical trials of new methods in use settings are essential to test their worth in developing countries and to select the best of several possible methods in a given setting. Approx. Increased Cost: $8 million annually.

2. <u>Long-term approaches</u>: Increased research toward better understanding of human reproductive physiology will lead to better methods of fertility control for use in five to fifteen years. A great deal has yet to be learned about basic aspects of male and female fertility and how regulation can be effected. For example, an -effective and safe male contraceptive is needed, in particular an injection which will be effective for specified periods of time. Fundamental research must be done but there are reasons to believe that the development of an injectable male contraceptive is feasible. Another method which should be developed is an injection which will assure a woman of regular periods. The drug would be given by pare-professionals once a month or as needed to regularize the menstrual cycle. Recent scientific advances indicate that this

method can be developed. Approx. Increased Cost: $20 million annually.

B. Development of Low-cost Delivery Systems

Discussion

Exclusive of China, only 10-15% of LDC populations are currently effectively reached by family planning activities. If efforts to reduce rapid population growth are to be successful it is essential that the neglected 85- 90% of LDC populations have access to convenient, reliable family planning services. Moreover, these people -- largely in rural but also in urban areas -- not only tend to have the highest fertility, they simultaneously suffer the poorest health, the worst nutritional levels, and the highest infant mortality rates.

Family planning services in LDCs are currently provided by the following means:

1. Government-run clinics or centers which offer family planning services alone;

2. Government-run clinics or centers which offer family planning as part of a broader based health service;

3. Government-run programs that emphasize door to door contact by family planning workers who deliver contraceptives to those desiring them and/or make referrals to clinics;

4. Clinics or centres run by private organizations (e.g., family planning associations);

5. Commercial channels which in many countries sell condoms, oral contraceptives, and sometimes spermicidal foam over the counter;

6.   Private physicians.

Two of these means in particular hold promise for allowing significant expansion of services to the neglected poor:

1. Integrated Delivery Systems. This approach involves the provision of family planning in conjunction with health and/or nutrition services, primarily through government-run programs. There are simple logistical reasons which argue for providing these services on an integrated basis. Very few of the LDCs have the resources, both in financial and manpower terms, to enable them to deploy individual types of services to the neglected 85% of their populations. By combining a variety of services in one delivery mechanism they can attain maximum impact with the scarce resources available.

In addition, the provision of family planning in the context of broader health services can help make family planning more acceptable to LDC leaders and individuals who, for a variety of reasons (some ideological, some simply humanitarian) object to family planning. Family planning in the health context shows a concern for the well-being of the family as a whole and not just for a couple's reproductive function.

Finally, providing integrated family planning and health services on a broad basis would help the U.S. contend with the ideological charge that the U.S. is more interested in curbing the numbers of LDC people than it is in their future and well-being. While it can be argued, and argued effectively, that limitation of numbers may well be one of the most critical factors in enhancing development potential and improving the chances for well-being, we should recognize that those who argue along ideological lines have made a great deal of the fact that the U.S. contribution to development programs and health programs has steadily shrunk, whereas funding for population programs has steadily increased. While many explanations may be brought forward to explain these trends, the fact is that they have been an ideological liability to the U.S. in its crucial developing relationships with the LDCs. A.I.D. currently spends about $35 million annually in bilateral programs on the provision of family planning services through integrated delivery systems. Any action to expand such systems must aim at the deployment of truly low- cost services. Health-related services which involve costly physical structures, high skill requirements, and expensive supply methods will not produce the desired deployment in any reasonable time. The basic test of low- cost methods will be whether the LDC governments concerned can assume responsibility for the financial, administrative, manpower and other elements of these service extensions. Utilizing existing indigenous structures and personnel (including traditional medical practitioners who in some countries have shown a strong interest in family planning) and service methods that involve simply-trained personnel, can help keep costs within LDC resource capabilities.

2.   Commercial Channels. In an increasing number of LDCs, contraceptives (such as condoms, foam and the Pill) are being made available without prescription requirements through commercial channels such as drugstores.* The commercial approach offers a practical, low-cost means of providing family planning services, since it utilizes an existing distribution system and does not involve financing the further expansion of public clinical delivery facilities. Both A.I.D. and private organizations like the IPPF are currently testing commercial distribution schemes in various LDCs to obtain further information on the feasibility, costs, and degree of family planning acceptance achieved through this approach. A.I.D. is currently spending about $2 million annually in this area.

In order to stimulate LDC provision of adequate family planning services, whether alone or in conjunction with health services, A.I.D. has subsidized contraceptive purchases for a number of years. In FY 1973 requests from A.I.D. bilateral and grantee programs for contraceptive supplies — in particular for oral contraceptives and condoms — increased markedly, and have continued to accelerate in FY 1974. Additional rapid expansion in demand is

---

* For obvious reasons, the initiative to distribute prescription drugs through commercial channels should be taken by local government and not by the US Government.

expected over the next several years as the accumulated population/family planning efforts of the past decade gain momentum.

While it is useful to subsidize provision of contraceptives in the short term in order to expand and stimulate LDC family planning programs, in the long term it will not be possible to fully fund demands for commodities, as well as other necessary family planning actions, within A.I.D. and other donor budgets. These costs must ultimately be borne by LDC governments and/or individual consumers. Therefore, A.I.D. will increasingly focus on developing contraceptive production and procurement capacities by the LDCs themselves. A.I.D. must, however, be prepared to continue supplying large quantities of contraceptives over the next several years to avoid a detrimental hiatus in program supply lines while efforts are made to expand LDC production and procurement actions. A.I.D. should also encourage other donors and multilateral organizations to assume a greater share of the effort, in regard both to the short-term actions to subsidize contraceptive supplies and the longer-term actions to develop LDC capacities for commodity production and procurement.

Recommendations:

1. A.I.D. should aim its population assistance program to help achieve adequate coverage of couples having the highest fertility who do not now have access to family planning services.

2. The service delivery approaches which seem to hold greatest promise of reaching these people should be vigorously pursued. For example:

    a. The U.S. should indicate its willingness to join with other donors and organizations to encourage further action by LDC governments and other institutions to provide low-cost family planning and health services to groups in their populations who are not now reached by such services. In accordance with Title X of the AID Legislation and current policy, A.I.D. should be prepared to provide substantial assistance in this area in response to sound requests.

    b. The services provided must take account of the capacities of the LDC governments or institutions to absorb full responsibility, over reasonable time-frames, for financing and managing the level of services involved.

c. A.I.D. and other donor assistance efforts should utilize to the extent possible indigenous structures and personnel in delivering services, and should aim at the rapid development of local (community) action and sustaining capabilities.

d. A.I.D. should continue to support experimentation with commercial distribution of contraceptives and application of useful findings in order to further explore the feasibility and replicability of this approach. Efforts in this area by other donors and organizations should be encouraged. Approx. U.S. Cost: $5-10 million annually.

3. In conjunction with other donors and organizations, A.I.D. should actively encourage the development of LDC capabilities for production and procurement of needed family planning contraceptives.

Special Footnote: While the agencies participating in this study have no specific recommendations to propose on abortion the following issues are believed important and should be considered in the context of a global population strategy.

Abortion

1. Worldwide Abortion Practices
   Certain facts about abortion need to be appreciated:

   -- No country has reduced its population growth without resorting to abortion.

   -- Thirty million pregnancies are estimated to be terminated annually by abortion throughout the world. The figure is a guess. More precise data indicate about 7 percent of the world's population live in countries where abortion is prohibited without exception and 12 percent in countries where abortion is permitted only to save the life of the pregnant woman. About 15 percent live under statutes authorizing abortion on broader medical grounds, that is, to avert a threat to the woman's health, rather than to her life, and sometimes on eugenic and/or juridical grounds (rape, etc.) as well. Countries where social factors may be taken into consideration to justify termination of pregnancy account for 22 percent of the world's population and those allowing for elective abortion for at least some categories of women, for 36 percent. No information is available for the remaining 8 percent; it would appear, however, that most of these people live in areas with restrictive abortion laws.

   -- The abortion statutes of many countries are not strictly enforced and some abortions on medical grounds are probably tolerated in most places. It is well known that in some countries with very restrictive laws, abortions can be obtained from physicians openly and without interference from the authorities. Conversely, legal authorization of elective abortion does not guarantee that abortion on request is actually available to all women who may want their pregnancies terminated. Lack of medical personnel and facilities or conservative attitudes among physicians and hospital administrators may effectively curtail access to abortion, especially for economically or socially deprived women.

2. U.S. Legislation and Policies Relative to Abortion

Although the Supreme Court of the United States invalidated the abortion laws of most states in January 1973, the subject still remains politically sensitive. U.S. Government actions relative to abortion are restricted as indicated by the following Federal legislation and the resultant policy decisions of the concerned departments and agencies.

a. A.I.D. Program

The predominant part of A.I.D.'s population assistance program has concentrated on contraceptive or foresight methods. A.I.D. recognized, however, that under developing country conditions foresight methods not only are frequently unavailable but often fail because of ignorance, lack of preparation, misuse and non-use. Because of these latter conditions, increasing numbers of women in the developing world have been resorting to abortion, usually under unsafe and often lethal conditions. Indeed, abortion, legal and illegal, now has become the most widespread fertility control method in use in the world today. Since, in the developing world, the increasingly widespread practice of abortion is conducted often under unsafe conditions, A.I.D. sought through research to reduce the health risks and other complexities which arise from the illegal and unsafe forms of abortion. One result has been the development of the Menstrual Regulation Kit, a simple, inexpensive, safe and effective means of fertility control which is easy to use under LDC conditions.

Section 114 of the Foreign Assistance Act of 1961 (P.L. 93-189), as amended in 1974, adds for the first time restrictions on the use of A.I.D. funds relative to abortion. The provision states that "None of the funds made available to carry out this part (Part I of the Act) shall be used to pay for the performance of abortions as a method of family planning or to motivate or coerce any person to practice abortions."

In order to comply with Section 114, A.I.D. has determined that foreign assistance funds will not be used to:

(i)   procure or distribute equipment provided for the purpose of inducing abortions as a method of family planning.

(ii)   directly support abortion activities in LDCs. However, A.I.D. may provide population program support to LDCs and institutions as long as A.I.D. funds are wholly attributable to the permissible aspects of such programs.

(iii)   information, education, training, or communication programs that promote abortion as a method of family planning. However, A.I.D. will continue to finance training of LDC doctors in the latest techniques used in obstetrics-gynaecology practice, and will not disqualify such training programs if they include pregnancy termination within the overall curriculum. Such training is provided only at the election of the participants.

(iiii)   pay women in the LDCs to have abortions as a method of family planning or to pay persons to perform abortions or to solicit persons to undergo abortions.

A.I.D. funds may continue to be used for research relative to abortion since the Congress specifically chose not to include research among the prohibited activities.

A major effect of the amendment and policy determination is that A.I.D. will not be involved in further development or promotion of the Menstrual Regulation Kit. However, other donors or organizations may become interested in promoting with their own funds dissemination of this promising fertility control method.

b. DHEW Programs

Section 1008 of the Family Planning Services and Population Research Act of 1970 (P.L. 91-572) states that "None of the funds appropriated under this title shall be used in programs where abortion is a method of family planning." DHEW has adhered strictly to the intent of Congress and does not support abortion research. Studies of the causes and consequences of abortion are permitted, however. The Public Health Service Act Extension of 1973 (P.L. 9345) contains the Church Amendment which establishes the right of health providers (both individuals and institutions) to refuse to perform an abortion if it conflicts with moral or religious principles.

c. Proposed Legislation on Abortion Research

There are numerous proposed Congressional amendments and bills which are more restrictive on abortion research than any of the pieces of legislation cited above.

It would be unwise to restrict abortion research for the following reasons:

1. The persistent and ubiquitous nature of abortion.

2. Widespread lack of safe abortion technique.

3. Restriction of research on abortifacient drugs and devices would:

a. Possibly eliminate further development of the IUD.

b. Prevent development of drugs which might have other beneficial uses. An example is methotrexate (R) which is now used to cure a hitherto fatal tumour of the uterus -- choriocarcinoma. This drug was first used as an abortifacient.

C. <u>Utilization of Mass Media and Satellite Communications Systems for Family Planning</u>

1. <u>Utilization of Mass Media for Dissemination of Family Planning Services and Information.</u>

The potential of education and its various media is primarily a function of (a) target populations where socio-economic conditions would permit reasonable people to change their behavior with the receipt of information about family planning and (b) the adequate development of the substantive motivating context of the message. While dramatic limitations in the availability of any family planning related message are most severe in rural areas of developing countries, even more serious gaps exist in the understanding of the implicit incentives in the system for large families and the potential of the informational message to alter those conditions.

Nevertheless, progress in the technology for mass media communications has led to the suggestion that the priority need might lie in the utilization of this technology, particularly with large and illiterate rural populations. While there are on-going efforts they have not yet reached their full potential. Nor have the principal U.S. agencies concerned yet integrated or given sufficient priority to family planning information and population programs generally.

Yet A.I.D.'s work suggests that radio, posters, printed material, and various types of personal contacts by health/family planning workers tend to be more cost-effective than television except in those areas (generally urban) where a TV system is already in place which reaches more than just the middle and upper classes. There is great scope for use of mass media, particularly in the initial stages of making people aware of the benefits of family planning and of services available; in this way mass media can effectively complement necessary interpersonal communications.

In almost every country of the world there are channels of communication (media) available, such, as print media, radio, posters, and personal contacts, which already reach the vast majority of the population. For example, studies in India - with only 30% literacy, show that most of the population is aware of the government's family planning program. If response is low it is not because of lack of media to transmit information.

A.I.D. believes that the best bet in media strategy is to encourage intensive use of media already available, or available at relatively low cost. For example, radio is a medium which in some countries already reaches a sizeable percentage of the rural population; a recent A.I.D.

financed study by Stanford indicates that radio is as effective as television, costs one-fifth as much, and offers more opportunities for programming for local needs and for local feedback.

Recommendations

USAID and USIA should encourage other population donors and organizations to develop comprehensive information and educational programs dealing with population and family planning consistent with the geographic and functional population emphasis discussed in other sections. Such programs should make use of the results of AID's extensive experience in this field and should include consideration of social, cultural and economic factors in population control as well as strictly technical and educational ones.

2. Use of U.S. broadcast satellites for dissemination of family planning and health information to key LDC countries

Discussion

One key factor in the effective use of existing contraceptive techniques has been the problem of education. In particular, this problem is most severe in rural areas of the developing countries. There is need to develop a cost-effective communications system designed for rural areas which, together with local direct governmental efforts, can provide comprehensive health information and in particular, family planning guidance. One new supporting technology which has been under development is the broadcast satellite. NASA and Fairchild have now developed an ATS (Applied Technology Satellite), now in orbit, which has the capability of beaming educational television programs to isolated areas via small inexpensive community receivers.

NASA's sixth Applications Technology Satellite was launched into geosynchronous orbit over the Galapagos Islands on May 30, 1974. It will be utilized for a year in that position to deliver health and educational services to millions of Americans in remote regions of the Rocky Mountain States, Alaska and Appalachia. During this period it will be made available for a short time to Brazil in order to demonstrate how such a broadcast satellite may be used to provide signals to 500 schools in their existing educational television network 1400 miles northeast of Rio de Janeiro in Rio Grande do Norte.

In mid-1975, ATS-6 will be moved to a point over the Indian Ocean to begin beaming educational television to India. India is now developing its broadcast program materials. Signals picked up from one of two Indian ground transmitters will be rebroadcast to individual stations in 2500 villages and to ground relay installations serving networks comprising 3000 more. This operation over India will last one year, after which time India hopes to have its own broadcast satellite in preparation.

Eventually it will be possible to broadcast directly to individual TV sets in remote rural areas. Such a "direct broadcast satellite," which is still under development, could one day go directly into individual TV receivers. At present, broadcast satellite signals go to ground receiving stations and are relayed to individual television sets on a local or regional basis. The latter can be used in towns, villages and schools.

The hope is that these new technologies will provide a substantial input in family planning programs, where the primary constraint lies in informational services. The fact, however, is that information and education does not appear to be the primary constraint in the development of effective family planning programs. AID itself has learned from costly intensive inputs that a supply oriented approach to family planning is not and cannot be fully effective until the demand side - incentives and motivations are both understood and accounted for.

Leaving this vast problem aside, AID has much relevant experience in the numerous problems encountered in the use of modern communications media for mass rural education. First, there is widespread LDC sensitivity to satellite broadcast, expressed most vigorously in the Outer Space Committee of the UN. Many countries don't want broadcasts of neighbouring countries over their own territory and fear unwanted propaganda and subversion by hostile broadcasters. NASA experience suggests that the U.S. must tread very softly when discussing assistance in program content. International restrictions may be placed on the types of proposed broadcasts and it remains technically difficult to restrict broadcast area coverage to national boundaries. To the extent programs are developed jointly and are appreciated and wanted by receiving countries, some relaxation in their position might occur.

Agreement is nearly universal among practitioners of educational technology that the technology is years ahead of software or content development. Thus cost per person reached tend to be very high. In addition, given the current technology, audiences are limited to those who are willing to walk to the village TV set and listen to public service messages and studies show declining audiences over time with large audiences primarily for popular entertainment. In addition, keeping village receivers in repair is a difficult problem. The high cost of program development remains a serious constraint, particularly since there is so little experience in validifying program content for wide general audiences.

With these factors it is clear that one needs to proceed slowly in utilization of this technology for the LDCs in the population field.

Recommendations:

1. The work of existing networks on population, education, ITV, and broadcast satellites should be brought together to better consolidate relative priorities for research, experimentation and programming in family planning. Wider distribution of the broad AID experience in these areas would probably be justified. This is particularly true since specific studies have already been done on the experimental ATS-6 programs in the U.S., Brazil, and India and each clearly documents the very experimental character and high costs of the effort. Thus at this point it is clearly inconsistent with U.S. or LDC population goals to allocate large additional sums for a technology which is experimental.

2. Limited donor and recipient family planning funds available for education/motivation must be allocated on a cost-effectiveness basis. Satellite TV may have opportunities for cost-effectiveness primarily where the decision has already been taken — on other than family planning grounds — to undertake very large-scale rural TV systems. Where applicable in such countries satellite technology should be used when cost-effective. Research should give special attention to costs and efficiency relative to alternative media.

3. Where the need for education is established and an effective format has been developed, we recommend more effective exploitation of existing and conventional media: radio, printed material, posters, etc., as discussed under part I above.

V. Action to Develop World-Wide Political and Popular Commitment to Population Stability

Discussion:

A far larger, high-level effort is needed to develop a greater commitment of leaders of both developed and developing countries to undertake efforts, commensurate with the need, to bring population growth under control.

In the United States, we do not yet have a domestic population policy despite widespread recognition that we should −− supported by the recommendations of the remarkable Report of the Commission on Population Growth and the American Future.

Although world population growth is widely recognized within the Government as a current danger of the highest magnitude calling for urgent measures, it does not rank high on the agendas of conversations with leaders of other nations.

Nevertheless, the United States Government and private organizations give more attention to the subject than any donor countries except, perhaps, Sweden, Norway and Denmark. France makes no meaningful contribution either financially or verbally. The USSR no longer opposes efforts of U.S. agencies but gives no support.

In the LDCs, although 31 countries, including China, have national population growth control programs and 16 more include family planning in their national health services — at least in some degree −− the commitment by the leadership in some of these countries is neither high nor wide. These programs will have only modest success until there is much stronger and wider acceptance of their real importance by leadership groups. Such acceptance and support will be essential to assure that the population information, education and service programs have vital moral backing, administrative capacity, technical skills and government financing.

Recommendations:

1. Executive Branch

    a. The President and the Secretary of State should make a point of discussing our national concern about world population growth in meetings with national leaders where it would be relevant.

    b. The Executive Branch should give special attention to briefing the Congress on population matters to stimulate support and leadership which the Congress has exercised in the past. A program for this purpose should be developed by S/PM with H and AID.

2. <u>World Population Conference</u>

    a.   In addition to the specific recommendations for action listed in the preceding sections, U.S. agencies should use the prestige of the World Population Plan of Action to advance all of the relevant action recommendations made by it in order to generate more effective programs for population growth limitation. AID should coordinate closely with the UNFPA in trying to expand resources for population assistance programs, especially from non-OECD, non-traditional donors.

        The U.S. should continue to play a leading role in ECOSOC and General Assembly discussions and review of the WPPA.

3. <u>Department of State</u>

    a.   The State Department should urge the establishment at U.N. headquarters of a high level seminar for LDC cabinet and high level officials and non-governmental leaders of comparable responsibility for indoctrination in population matters. They should have the opportunity in this seminar to meet the senior officials of U.N. agencies and leading population experts from a variety of countries.

    b.   The State Department should also encourage organization of a UNFPA policy staff to consult with leaders in population programs of developing countries and other experts in population matters to evaluate programs and consider actions needed to improve them.

    c.   A senior officer, preferably with ambassadorial experience, should be assigned in each regional bureau dealing with LDCs or in State's Population Office to give full-time attention to the development of commitment by LDC leaders to population growth reduction.

    d.   A senior officer should be assigned to the Bureau of International Organization Affairs to follow and press action by the Specialized Agencies of the U.N. in population matters in developing countries.

    e.   Part of the present temporary staffing of S/PM for the purposes of the World Population Year and the World Population Conference should be continued on a permanent basis to take advantage of momentum gained by the Year and Conference.

<u>Alternate View on 3.c.</u>

    b.   The Department should expand its efforts to help Ambassadorial and other high-ranking U.S.G. personnel understand the consequences of rapid population growth and the remedial measures possible.

    c.   The Department would also give increased attention to developing a commitment to population growth reduction on the part of LDC leaders.

    d.   Adequate manpower should be provided inS/PM and other parts of the Department as appropriate to implement these expanded efforts.

4.   A I D. should expand its programs to increase the understanding of LDC leaders regarding the consequences of rapid population growth and their commitment to undertaking remedial actions. This should include necessary actions for collecting and analyzing adequate and reliable demographic data to be used in promoting awareness of the problem and in formulating   appropriate policies and programs.

5.   USIA. As a major part of U.S. information policy, the improving but still limited programs of USIA to convey information on population matters should be strengthened to a level commensurate with the importance of the subject.

(END OF NSSM 200)

National Security Council

Memorandum (NSSM) 314

November 26, 1975

CPSIA information can be obtained
at www.ICGtesting.com
Printed in the USA
BVHW060509061122
650971BV00001B/27